WHEN THE
MOON
SLIPS AWAY

Rejoicing in Everyday Miracles

MELANNIE SVOBODA, SND

When the
MOON
Slips Away

*Rejoicing in
Everyday Miracles*

TWENTY
THIRD *23rd*
PUBLICATIONS

Dedication

To Mary and Charlene Svoboda,
not only my sisters-in-law,
but also my good friends.

TWENTY-THIRD PUBLICATIONS
A Division of Bayard
One Montauk Avenue, Suite 200
New London, CT 06320
(860) 437-3012 or (800) 321-0411
www.23rdpublications.com

ISBN 978-1-58595-728-6
Library of Congress Catalog Card Number: 2008940047

Printed in the U.S.A.

Contents

Introduction

This book is meant for anyone (like me) who loves nature. It is meant for anyone (like me) who believes that one of the primary ways we come to know God is through the created world. It is meant for anyone (like me) who never tires of learning more and more about the fascinating universe of which we are a part.

In a previous book, *When the Rain Speaks*, I celebrated God's presence in nature through a wide variety of natural phenomena such as rain, trees, mountains, giraffes, owls, bees, flowers, the sun, photosynthesis, and the cosmos. In this book I continue the celebration with reflections on other facets of the natural world such as the moon, the wind, dogs, tulips, newly hatched chicks, the desert, sleep, the human thumb, evaporation, the Grand Canyon, and orca the whale.

Each chapter begins with a thought-provoking quotation from a wide variety of sources. Each includes several questions for personal reflection and/or communal sharing followed by an appropriate quotation from Scripture. And finally, each chapter concludes with a short prayer that flows from the reflection.

I believe we are swimming in a sea of mystery called creation. Sadly, we are often blind to the beauty surrounding us and inside of us. We often pay scant heed to the miracles in our everyday lives, because these miracles masquerade as the commonplace or the expected. Fyodor Dostoevsky, the great Russian writer, said this about the world of nature: "Love all God's creation, both the whole and every grain of sand. Love every leaf, every ray of light. Love the animals, love the plants, love each separate thing." If you do this, he says, "You will pierce the mystery of God in all…until you come at last to love the whole world with a love that will be all-embracing and eternal." It is my hope that this book, in one small way, may foster your love for all of creation, a love that will lead you to pierce the mystery of God in everything.

1

Take a Walk with a Little Child

Do not say, "It is morning," and dismiss it with the name of yesterday. See it for the first time as a newborn child that has no name.

~ RABINDRANATH TAGORE

A man who has collected thousands of arrowheads once said, "If you really want to find arrowheads, you must walk with a child—a child will pick up everything." A child will not only pick up everything, a child will first see everything. A child is not like us jaded adults who, because we have walked this planet for many years, think we have seen all there is to see, and we know all there is to know. You'll never catch a child saying, "Been there. Done that." At least not a young child.

I was sitting in a park one day when a man came by carrying his young son, a toddler. He stopped where a large expanse of lawn was spread out before them. The little boy began to squirm in the man's arms. Obviously he wanted to be put down. The man obliged. As soon as he did, the little boy sat down on the grass and began stroking it with both hands. He giggled when he did this—as if the feel of the grass were intoxicating. The father plopped down next to the boy and began to stroke the grass too—as if he too were feeling it for the first time.

Then the toddler pulled a few clumps of grass and began to examine them more closely with a serious expression on his face. The father took a blade, cupped it in his hands, and blew: HONK! The child giggled at the noise the grass made. Next the little boy got up and started running down the gentle slope of the lawn, his father in careful pursuit. I remember thinking, "That child is re-acquainting his father with the beauty and mystery of grass! That father is seeing grass anew through the eyes of his little boy."

In her book *The Natural History of the Senses*, Diane Ackerman writes, "...how thickly demanding just being alive is." She goes on to explain that life is so complex that our brains would be overwhelmed with messages if our senses noticed everything. We would be exhausted just by being alive. So, as a kind of self-defense, the senses do not report everything to the brain that they see, smell, touch, taste, or feel. Otherwise we would go mad just feeling the clothes on our backs all day or hearing every single sound that registered on our eardrums.

Instead the senses look for general patterns ("The sun is rising again—as it should. I don't have to pay attention to it because it comes up every day.") and for novelty ("Look at that purple bird!"), and simply ignore many of the other stimuli they receive. Once the senses have experienced something—like grass or a sunrise or a parakeet—these things become commonplace, and we find ourselves saying, "Oh, that again," or "That's old hat." As a result, says Ackerman, "Much of our life passes in a comfortable blur. Living on the senses requires an easily triggered sense of marvel, a little extra energy, and most people are lazy about life." Perhaps only artists, mystics, and children live life at this deep level of marvel.

So, when we think we know it all, or when we feel disconnected from the world in which we live, or when we're feeling blue, or when we sense we are taking everything for granted, then that is a good time to read a poem, recite a prayer of a mystic, visit an art museum, or take a walk with a little child.

Reflection • Discussion

Have I ever seen the world anew through the eyes of a child? If so, what was the experience like for me?

Is my sense of marvel easily triggered or is it easily dulled?

What can I do to see the world through the eyes of an artist, mystic, or child today?

> Jesus called a child over, placed it in their midst, and said, "Amen, I say to you, unless you turn and become like children, you will not enter the kingdom of heaven."
>
> — MATTHEW 18:2–3

 Lover of children, let me see the world today with the eyes of a child.

2

All about Dogs

The average dog is a nicer person than the average person.

O f all the animals in the world, only the dog has earned the sobriquet "man's best friend." Of course, the dog can be woman's and child's best friend too. The dog (called *canis lupus familians* by biologists) is almost universally loved all over the world. There are a few places where dogs are held in contempt, but we needn't dwell on those. The popularity of dogs is demonstrated simply by the fact that there are an estimated 400 million dogs in the world today.

One thing that makes dogs so popular is the wide variety of shapes, sizes, and colors they come in. There's a dog to suit everyone's taste. Kennel clubs worldwide officially recognize over 800 breeds, but there are also countless mixed-breeds which we call disparagingly (or affectionately) curs, mongrels, mutts, pavement specials, or Heinz 57s. Dogs range in size from teeny (the Chihuahua weighs under six pounds) to humongous (the Great Dane can weigh over 200 pounds.) Their colors vary from white to black with an array of grays and browns too. Sometimes their coats are one solid color, while other times they are multi-colored, often with attractive or unique patterns. I recently saw a small white dog on TV with black markings that spelled out I–❤-U. Dogs' fur can be long, short, or in between; it can be coarse, soft, straight, wavy, or curly. In other words, Toto (a cairn terrier) looks nothing like Lassie (a rough collie).

Dogs are a sub-species of the wolf. Though domesticated, dogs retain some of their wolf-like characteristics. They are predators and scavengers with sharp teeth and strong jaws for attacking and ripping apart their food, your sneaker, or a burglar's ankle. Like wolves, dogs are also highly social. What looks like loyalty and devotion to their human owners is really part of the dog's natural instinct as a pack animal. The first dogs were domesticated in eastern Asia (probably China) about 15,000 years ago. Since then, we humans have used dogs to help us with our work, to afford us protection, and to provide us with companionship.

Because dogs are so familiar to us, it is easy to assume we know everything there is to know about them. Here are a few facts about dogs that you might not know:

1. The Hindus worship dogs as part of a five-day festival called Tihar.

2. In Chinese astrology, the dog is one of twelve animals honored.

3. Dogs have a great range of hearing—as low as 16Hz (com-

pared to 20 Hz for humans) and as high as 45 kHz (compared to 20 kHz for humans).

4. Dogs have sweat glands in their paws.

5. Some dogs go around in a circle several times before lying down. This is one of their left over wolf traits. In the wild, they would have to pack down the grass before lying down for the night. Even though most domesticated dogs no longer sleep in wild grass, many have retained this peculiar little habit.

6. Dogs can have nearly 220 million smell-sensitive cells in their noses, whereas humans have only 5 million.

7. Dogs have been trained to help humans in a variety of areas: search and rescue; law enforcement; guarding livestock, people, and property; herding animals; hunting; guiding the seeing and hearing impaired; and doing therapy work in hospitals and nursing homes.

There is even a patron saint of dogs: St. Roch (also known as St. Rock) who lived in fourteenth-century France and Italy. According to legend, St. Roch had miraculous powers of healing people of the black plague. But when he himself was stricken with the disease, he retreated to the woods to die. Here's where the story gets interesting. One version says a man name Gothard discovered the saint's retreat and nursed him back to health. But another version says it was a dog that befriended the saint, licked his sores, brought him food from his master's table, and nursed him back to health. You can pick whatever version appeals to you the most. I, for one, am opting for the dog.

Reflection • Discussion

Are there any dogs in my life that made an impact on me—positively or negatively?

Have any dogs helped me or provided me with companionship?

"And lying at his door was a poor man named Lazarus, covered with sores, who would gladly have eaten his fill of the scraps that fell from the rich man's table. Dogs even used to come and lick his sores." — LUKE 16:20–21

I thank you, God, for all those beings (including dogs) who have been companions with me on my journey in life.

3

The Moon Is Always Whole

As thou has set the moon in the sky to be
the poor man's lantern, so let thy Light
shine in my dark life and lighten my path.

❧ ANONYMOUS INDIAN PRAYER

The moon is the earth's only natural satellite. Although we humans have a propensity for naming anything and everything, we have given no formal name to the moon. We just call it the moon. Yet we have given all kinds of names to the moons of the other planets. Ganymede is the name we've given to the largest of Jupiter's sixty-three moons, for example, and Titan the name of the largest of Saturn's fifty-six moons. Maybe since earth has only one moon, we feel there is no reason to give our moon a special name. When we say, "Hey, look at the moon!" everyone knows which moon we are talking about.

Our moon, which is roughly one-third the size of earth, is about 238,900 miles away from us. It orbits the earth every 27.3 days. The moon also rotates on its axis, but because it rotates synchronously, it keeps nearly the same side turned toward the earth all the time. That's part of the moon's mystique. We never see its other side. Another part of the moon's mystique is the way its gravitational pull affects the earth. The moon's pull is largely responsible for the tides of the earth. But some people maintain the moon's gravitational pull affects our planet in other ways too—such as causing strange behavior in humans. Over the years I have known many a teacher who claimed she could chart the phases of the moon simply by observing the behavior of her students.

As you would expect, scientists have studied the moon very thoroughly. They seem especially fascinated by the moon's craters and have even given them names. The South Pole-Aitken Basin is not only the largest crater on the moon, it is the largest known crater in our solar system. Many ancient people considered the moon a deity. In the fifth century B.C., the Greek philosopher Amaxagoras got into trouble when he taught that the moon was no god or goddess, but was actually a spherical rock that reflected light from the sun. He was imprisoned and eventually exiled for teaching such nonsense.

For centuries humans dreamed of going to the moon. In 1959 the first man-made object impacted the moon's surface when the Soviet Union sent Luna 2 to the moon. The dream of humans on the moon was realized in 1969 when the United States successfully put two men on the moon. A total of six manned flights to the moon occurred between 1969 and 1972. At present there is talk of setting up a permanent base there.

Although there are several US flags and the Soviet coat of arms on the moon, international treaties prevent any nation from claiming the moon. Instead, the moon is treated legally like international waters. The Outer Space Treaty further restricts the use of the moon to peaceful purposes, specifically banning any weapons of mass destruction. Ironically, it is safer to live on the moon than on earth!

All these facts about the moon, though interesting to many, cannot compare with simply enjoying the moon. There is beauty and mystery in its different phases from thin crescent to round fullness. There is beauty in the moon's various sizes from huge (when it is close to the horizon) to merely ornamental when it is high in the sky. The moon seems to change colors too: white, whitish yellow, yellow, yellowish blue, blue, bluish gray, gray, to name a few. And remember, no matter what color the moon is, its light is all borrowed light from the sun.

Barbara Kingsolver has written a lovely poem entitled "Remember the Moon Survives." In it she reminds us that despite the moon's waxing and waning, the moon is always whole. Though the moon seems to slip away at times, it is always there. Even when it seems to disappear altogether, it is always fully present. I find this thought very consoling when I apply it to my spiritual life. At times, God's presence in my life seems to slip away or disappear altogether. When this happens, I recall the moon. And I remind myself that God's presence in my life is like the moon—always whole, always fully here.

At the same time, writer F. Lynne Bachleda warns against trying too hard "to squeeze the divine" out of every aspect of nature. She calls such attempts "a misapplication of effort." Rather she says, "the rescue of beauty, texture, sound, heat, and light saturates and saves us, whether we know it or not." In other words, though the moon can be a metaphor for the divine in our life, we can enjoy it just for what it is: a lovely phenomenon of the natural world. The beauty of the moon with its textured surface, changing colors, varied phases, steady rotation and gravitational pull is saving us, whether we know it or not.

Reflection • Discussion

Did I learn anything new in this chapter?

Does the moon intrigue me? Why or why not?

How does the moon speak to me or to my spiritual life?

> God made the two great lights, the greater one to govern the day, and the lesser one to govern the night.
>
> — GENESIS 1:16

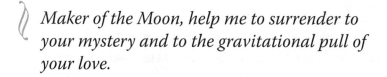 *Maker of the Moon, help me to surrender to your mystery and to the gravitational pull of your love.*

4

Mechtild and Francis

My soul can find no staircase to Heaven
unless it be through Earth's loveliness.

☞ MICHELANGELO BUONARROTI

echtild of Magdeburg was a thirteenth-century mystic from Saxony. Many of her writings are filled with nature imagery. She addresses God as Burning Mountain, Fathomless Well, Chosen Sun, Perfect Moon, Unattainable Height. She once referred to herself as "a dusty acre" in need of "the fruitful rain of Christ's humanity, and the gentle dew of the Spirit." She is said to have received many revelations from God during her long hours at prayer and, urged by her spiritual director to write them down, she filled six volumes. Yet she could say, "Of the heavenly things God has shown me, I can speak but a little, no more than a honeybee can carry away on its foot from an overflowing jar."

Mechtild's images are more than quaint. They are strong. They are vivid. They ring true. They support the premise that God often speaks to us through the components and patterns of our everyday life. And what is occurring in the deepest recesses of our soul is often best expressed through images drawn from the natural world.

St. Francis of Assisi, a twelfth-century Italian saint, also loved nature. In fact, he is the patron saint of animals, birds, and ecology. There are many stories about his interaction with animals. One charming one says that as he was traveling with some companions one day, they came upon several trees filled with birds. Frances excused himself, saying he had to stop and preach to the birds. To the amazement of his companions, the birds did not fly away when Francis approached them. On the contrary, they seemed mesmerized by his voice. Francis told them, "My sister birds, you owe much to God, and you must always and in every place give praise to Him, for He has given you freedom to wing through the sky and He has clothed you."

Among Francis' writings is his famous "Canticle to the Sun" in which he thanks God for Brother Sun, Sister Moon, Brother Fire, Brothers Wind and Air, and Sister Water. Another legend also says that one day Francis walked by a rose bush in full bloom and said to it, "Stop shouting!"

John Powell, SJ, writes that the deepest mode of existence in creation is the presence of God whose being is reflected and shared in all of nature. He concludes, "God's pulse is the heart beat of the universe." Both Mechtild and Francis knew this. And lived it.

Reflection • Discussion

Do any of the words of Mechtild or Francis speak to me today?

What other aspects of nature reflect God to me?

What images from nature would I use to describe my current state of soul?

> The Lord is my light and my salvation;
>   whom do I fear?
> The Lord is my life's refuge;
>   of whom am I afraid?   — PSALM 27:1

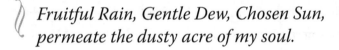

Fruitful Rain, Gentle Dew, Chosen Sun,
permeate the dusty acre of my soul.

5

Listening

The larger the island of knowledge,
the longer the shoreline of wonder.

☛ RALPH W. SOCKMAN

A retired doctor said recently that the most important diagnostic tool a doctor has is listening. He said, "The doctor must first sit with the patient, ask the right questions, and really listen to what the patient says." He fears that too many doctors are losing the art of listening simply because they are seeing too many patients. Or sometimes they are too eager to let their wonderful machines do all the diagnosing for them.

The problem with listening goes far beyond the doctor's office. We all risk losing this vital skill. Why? For one thing we are bombarded by way too many words each day. Wherever we go we cannot escape them—whether watching TV in our homes, attending a meeting at work, conversing with friends or acquaintances, listening to the radio in our cars, talking on our cell phones, or try-ing to shop where loud music or (worse yet) annoying commer-cials blare continuously. And it's not just the assault of words that threatens our ability to listen. It's all the other noises too: honking horns, screeching traffic, roaring airplanes, rackety dishwashers, banging furnaces, sputtering air conditioners, barking dogs. This constant bombardment of words and noises may be hindering our ability to listen to the things that really matter. Like what?

Like one another. Psychologists tell us many people are starv-ing for someone to listen to them. In fact, good psychologists are effective primarily because they are trained in the art of really listening to their clients and in reflecting back to them what they hear. They need to reflect back what they hear, because, the truth is, many of us do not even listen to ourselves! One of the first signs that a relationship is in trouble is when one or both of the parties say, "You aren't listening to what I'm saying!"

We need to listen to nature too. In her book, *The Listening God*, Miriam Pollard, a Carmelite nun, says people of ancient times had a different attitude toward nature than we do. For the ancients, "Nature was not objective, mechanical. It did not hap-pen. It spoke to you. You did not study it; you listened to it." Per-haps we moderns need to take time not only to smell the roses, but also to listen to them.

I often direct retreatants to go outside and listen to nature—a bluebird, a spruce tree, a creek, the clouds. One Sister returned after listening to the grass. She said she heard the grass say to her: "My beauty is not just in me singly, but also in being together to form a beautiful lawn…People don't like me unless I am green. My brown period doesn't mean that I am dead; I am just in my dormant stage. I am also beautiful then, just waiting." You might want to try listening to the grass yourself—or to a tree or rock or bird or squirrel or the ocean. Simply ask the natural object, "What wisdom can you share with me?" And listen. Really listen. You might be surprised at what you hear!

God is an excellent listener. This is one reason we are drawn to prayer, to share with God what is on our minds and in our hearts. Sister Miriam writes, "The listening heart of God draws out of us this wisdom [God] has been sowing in us all along. We need to speak to [God] in order to know what we already think we know."

Yes, prayer is about God listening to us. But it is also about us listening to God. And how does God speak to us? God often speaks precisely through the other people in our lives, through the natural world around us, through sacred Scripture, through current events, and through the deepest longings and whisperings of our souls. Shhh! Listen!

Reflection • Discussion

How well do I listen to the natural world?

How well do I listen to other people?

What are some of the deepest longings of my soul?

I will listen for the Word of God.   — PSALM 85:9

 Listening God, teach me to listen.

6

Skunks, Killdeer, and Bluegills

The care of the earth is our most ancient and worthy, and, after all, our most pleasing responsibility. To cherish what remains of it and to foster its renewal is our only hope.

☙ WENDELL BERRY

Sometimes people ask me, "Where did you get your love and respect for nature?" I am quick to respond, "Mostly from my parents." As I was growing up on our small farm in northeast Ohio, I saw ample evidence of my parents' great appreciation and respect for nature. Looking back on my father, these three incidents immediately come to mind.

The first one concerns skunks. While my father was tearing down the old barn on our farm, he came upon a mother skunk and her four little babies. Common sense told my father to get rid of the skunks or we would have many summer nights disturbed by their foul odor. But my father couldn't bring himself to do it. Instead he halted the demolition of the barn long enough for the mother skunk to move her little ones to a safe new home. "They're so cute," he mused as he watched her carrying her young skunks away one at a time. Sure enough, later that summer we were awakened quite a few nights by the overpowering smell of those five skunks. When we complained, my father only said, "Well, that's a small price to pay for living in the country."

The second incident concerned some killdeer. Each spring my father plowed several acres of our property for his garden. One time as he was plowing, he saw a pair of killdeer shrieking and skittering about, obviously in great distress. He stopped the tractor, got off, and walked around the unplowed section of the field. Sure enough, there it was: a killdeer's nest on the ground. It was not much of a dwelling, just a couple of stones on the ground with four black speckled eggs nestled in between. Instead of plowing the nest under, my father took a big stick and stuck it into the ground next to the nest. He got back on the tractor and continued to plow—carefully avoiding the area where the nest was.

The third incident involved some fish. My sister had a pond in front of her home with a small creek nearby. One day when we were visiting her family, my father decided to take a walk with his grandkids to check out the pond. To their dismay, they saw a handful of bluegills trapped in the shallow water of the creek. It seems that a storm the night before had caused the pond to overflow into the creek, carrying several fish with it. Now the fish were trapped in this small puddle of water struggling to breathe. My father took quick action. He carefully picked up the fish one at a time and deposited them back into the pond. But before letting them go, he swished them gently back and forth in the pond water for a few seconds. He had read somewhere that this is how you give artificial respiration to fish by forcing water over their gills. That day my father, with his grandkids, saved several bluegills from certain death.

Skunks, killdeer, and bluegills. Through these three incidents I learned much from my father. 1) Sometimes we humans must be willing to pay a price for living in harmony with nature. 2) Animals have just as much of a right to reproduce and extend their species into the future as humans do. 3) Even so-called lowly animals deserve a second chance at life—even if it means taking the trouble to perform emergency first-aid on them.

Reflection • Discussion

From whom did I get my love and appreciation for nature? How?

Do I agree with the introductory quotation? Why or why not?

What price am I willing to pay to live in harmony with nature?

> God blessed them, saying, "…Have dominion over the fish of the sea, the birds of the air, and all living things that move on the earth." — GENESIS 1:28

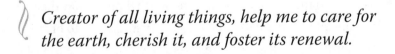

Creator of all living things, help me to care for the earth, cherish it, and foster its renewal.

7

The Great Red Spot on Jupiter

I wonder why. I wonder why I wonder.
I wonder why I wonder why I wonder.

☙ RICHARD FREYMAN

Jupiter is the largest planet in our solar system, the fifth planet from the sun. It is approximately 317 times the size of the earth, or 2½ times the size of all the other planets combined. Astronomers have nicknamed Jupiter "the great gas giant" because it is composed of 90% hydrogen and 10% helium, with dabs of methane, ammonia, and a few other things thrown in. Whether Jupiter has a core of heavier elements is not known for sure. In fact, much about Jupiter we don't know for sure.

The outer atmosphere of Jupiter is visibly separated into distinct broad bands of different latitudes. These various bands give rise to turbulent storms along their borders. One such storm is called the Great Red Spot.

The Great Red Spot (which is oval in shape) was first spotted on Jupiter by astronomer Robert Hooke in 1664. A year later, another astronomer, Giovanni Domenico Cassini, described a similar red spot—only his spot was in a different location than Hooke's. Throughout the centuries other scientists observed the red spot on Jupiter—most notably in 1830 and 1879. The big question though is this: Were they all seeing the same red spot? We don't know for sure. But many astronomers believe the red spot cited by Cassini—or at least the one noted in 1830—is the same one visible today. If so, that means this storm on Jupiter has been raging for close to 200 years or maybe even for almost 400 years. What storm on earth can claim such longevity?

On February 25, 1979, the United States launched Voyager 1, a space probe designed to get a closer look at Jupiter. When Voyager 1 was 5.7 million miles from Jupiter, it transmitted the first images of the Great Red Spot back to earth. Piecing together the data from Voyager 1 and other subsequent probes into space, astronomers have learned more about this incredible storm. The storm is massive—at least by earth standards. It is roughly 12,500 miles wide and could swallow up two or three earths. Scientists estimate that the winds of the storm are traveling 250 miles per hour. (Hurricanes on earth seldom exceed 180 miles per hour). They also noted that the spot is getting smaller and predict that, by 2040, it will be more circular than oval.

Is the Great Red Spot a gigantic hurricane? No. It is a high pressure storm (an anti-cyclonic storm), that rotates counterclockwise about every six earth days. Hurricanes on earth are low pressure storms. They often dissipate once they come ashore. One reason the Great Red Spot has lasted so long, then, is because it never goes over any land. Scientists offer a few other possible reasons for its longevity, but we don't know for sure why it has lasted so long. Why is the Great Red Spot red? Astronomers suspect its color (which ranges from brick-red to pale salmon) might be due to certain compounds of phosphorous, but (once again) we don't know for sure.

The Great Red Spot is truly a wonder in our universe. As one writer said, "We understand the broad properties but not all the detailed features of this remarkable phenomenon." In other words, we know some things about the Great Red Spot, but there are still many things we have yet to learn.

Reflection • Discussion

How much did I know about the Great Red Spot before I read this chapter?

What effect, if any, does knowledge of the sheer size and duration of this storm have on me personally?

Name some other things we don't know for sure about.

> Then the Lord addressed Job out of the storm and
> said…"Where were you when I founded the earth?
> Tell me, if you have understanding. Who determined
> its size? Do you know?"   — JOB 38:1, 4–5

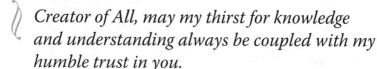

*Creator of All, may my thirst for knowledge
and understanding always be coupled with my
humble trust in you.*

8

Risk

*Any life truly lived is a risky business, and
if one puts up too many fences against the
risks, one ends by shutting out life itself.*
　　　　　　　　　　　◆ KENNETH S. DAVIS

We humans sometimes assume that most animals (be they lions or wasps) are ferocious. We picture them prowling around like hoodlum gang members itching for a fight. In reality, most animals spend quite a bit of their time just trying to avoid detection. An aggressive animal is probably hungry, protecting its young, or looking for a mate.

In fact, those are the three times most animals take risks: for food, for family, for fun (the sexual kind). Deer will leave the shelter of the forest and venture out into the open field in order to eat some tasty apples. The hungrier the deer are, the more risks they take. In winter where I live, deer will come all the way up onto people's patios and decks in search of food. One winter night, I saw several deer in our convent courtyard standing on their hind legs nibbling the branches of several young trees. Fish also forsake the security of the lake depths in search of food. And birds alight on the ground—a very dangerous place for them to be—in order to snatch a few fallen seeds. Hunger forces animals to take risks.

So do offspring. I was strolling near a lake one day in spring. A woman with a small white dog on a long leash was coming towards me. The dog pranced merrily along, oblivious to the trouble that was brewing. Suddenly, from across the lake, I heard a honking and loud commotion. The woman and I looked over and saw this huge goose (a gander) running across the surface of the lake. He was not trying to fly. He just kept skimming the water, coming straight at us. At first we were so shocked, we froze in our tracks. What in the world had we done to provoke this goose? Why had he become so ferocious? Suddenly we realized that his target was not us two ladies, it was the dog. As soon as the woman realized this, she screamed, scooped the pooch into her arms, and started running away from the goose as fast as she could. Fortunately, when the goose saw them fleeing, he put on his brakes. He came out of the water, though, and kept eyeing them, moving his head up and down in a menacing manner, until the woman with the dog had disappeared over the horizon. Satisfied, he flapped his wings a few times, smoothed his ruffled feathers, slipped back into the water, and swam to the other side of the lake—where (I saw later) his mate was sitting on a nest of eggs. Being a parent sometimes makes animals (including the human kind) do strange and risky things.

Then there is the risk involved in mating. Mating for many species is a dangerous business. I am not referring only to black widow spiders either. Contrary to popular lore, the female black widow does not always eat her mate after a night of frantic sex. Only occasionally—when she mistakes him for prey. But there are other ways mating is dangerous. Consider the cricket. When male crickets get in the mood for love, they begin to chirp. It is amazing how loud their chirp can be considering how small they are. The female crickets find this chirping alluring and will respond amorously to the sexiest chirper. But there is a big problem with chirping. It attracts not only potential mates, but also potential predators. As a result, some poor cricket swains are eaten by predators before they ever get a chance to consummate their love. Male lightning bugs are in the same predicament. Their blinking attracts not only the ladies, but also predators (and children with mason jars!)

Other species have risky behaviors during mating seasons. Frogs croak. Grouse males dance like there's no tomorrow (looking a little like your Uncle Harry at your niece's wedding.) The vigorous vocal display of male gibbons during courtship makes them easy prey for poachers who kill them and sell their body parts for traditional medicines. The actual act of mating is risky business for some species. I will not go into detail. Let me just say that one reason artificial insemination is so popular among horse breeders (besides the obvious convenience of not having to cart horses hither and yon), is because it protects both the mare and the stallion from possible injury during sex. I have no idea how the horses feel about this.

It is not a stretch of the imagination to see parallels in the world of humans. Like our animal confreres, we too have hungers—and many of them are not merely for food. We hunger for intimacy, excitement, knowledge, peace, security, fulfillment, even God. What are we willing to risk to satisfy some of these hungers? We are also programmed for relationships—not all of them of a sexual nature. Relationships are risky for humans. Maybe we will not be eaten by the other person, but we could be taken advantage of or even rejected. And finally, we humans can also be very loving toward and protective of our offspring, as well we should be. It is very risky to bring another human being into the world with all the responsibilities that go along with that. But for many people, it obviously is well worth the risk.

Reflection • Discussion

What are some of the risks I have taken in my life and why? Have they been worth it?

What are some of my deepest hungers?

Is God calling me to take other risks at this time in my life?

> Jesus said to him, "If you wish to be perfect, go, sell what you have and give it to the poor, and you will have treasure in heaven. Then come, follow me."
> — MATTHEW 19:21

 God, help me to be a risk taker in my continual quest for you.

9

My Mother and Her African Violets

If I had two loaves of bread, I would sell one and buy hyacinths, for they would feed my soul.

         ☙ KORAN

My mother was good at raising African violets. She always had several pots of them in the living room in all the homes in which she lived. I have concluded that there were two secrets for her success with African violets. First, she talked to them. Every time she watered them, she would speak sweetly and encouragingly to them, saying things like: "And how are you today, Honey? My, my! Aren't you pretty! Here's a nice big drink for you!" While she was talking to them, she would also unobtrusively pinch off any dry or shriveling leaves.

Whenever visitors complimented my mother on her violets, she would say, "They all had to learn to thrive on neglect." That was her second secret. She never fussed over her plants. She never fretted over whether they were getting the proper amount of sunlight or whether she was feeding them the right kind of plant food. Reflecting back on this, I think my mother entrusted most of the growth of her violets to the God who created them—or at least to the violets themselves. By doing so, she achieved a healthy relationship with her plants, a delicate balance that avoided both stifling control and thoughtless disregard. The plants, in turn, repaid her with lush blossoms in a profusion of colors: white, pink, lavender, blue, magenta, and purple.

The famous pianist-comedian Victor Borge once told a friend he was going to raise a few chickens. His friend protested, "But you don't know the first thing about raising chickens!" Borge replied, "I know I don't. But the chickens do."

Reflection • Discussion

How do I tend to the living things under my care?

Where am I on the spectrum between stifling control and thoughtless disregard?

> Jesus said, "Can you by worrying add a moment to your life-span? If even the smallest things are beyond your control, why are you anxious about the rest? Notice how the flowers grow." — LUKE 12:25–27

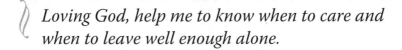

Loving God, help me to know when to care and when to leave well enough alone.

10

George Washington Carver

Wonder is the root of knowledge.

☛ ABRAHAM HESCHEL

*B*y all standards, George Washington Carver was a great man. Born into slavery in Diamond Grove, Mississippi, in the spring of 1864, George was kidnapped by raiders as an infant and, along with his mother, was sold in Arkansas. His original owner, Moses Carver, eventually found the boy, orphaned and near death, and brought him back to Diamond Grove. As a child, George developed respiratory problems that made him unable to work as a hand. Instead he spent much of his time exploring the fields and studying the wide variety of wild plants that grew in the area. Soon he became so knowledgeable about the medicinal properties of plants that he was dubbed "Doctor George."

After slavery was abolished, Carver learned to read and write. Eventually he went to college, becoming the first black student at Iowa State University. For forty-seven years he taught and conducted research at Tuskegee University where Booker T. Washington also worked. Most of Carver's research was aimed at helping poor farmers in the south whose soil had been ruined from years of growing only cotton. Carver encouraged crop rotation. He also studied specific plants such as sweet potatoes, soybeans, and peanuts.

Carver is credited with developing hundreds of applications for these crops—most notably the peanut. Although criticized for not keeping records or writing out his formulas, he supposedly developed 300 uses for peanuts alone, including bleach, metal polish, printer's ink, glue for postage stamps, cooking oils, shaving cream, mayonnaise, cloth dyes, wood stains, and (of course) peanut butter. Carver sought no patents for his food products because he believed food plants were to be used as gifts from God and, therefore, they should never be patented for personal or commercial gain.

Carver received numerous honors and awards during his lifetime. On January 5, 1943, he died at the age of seventy-nine after falling down a flight of stairs. The epitaph on his tombstone reads: "He could have added fortune to fame, but caring for neither, he found happiness and honor in being helpful to the world."

Reflection • Discussion

What struck me the most about Carver?

Do I think food should be patented? Why or why not?

Do I find "happiness and honor in being helpful to the world"?

Stand and consider the wondrous works of God!

— JOB 37:14

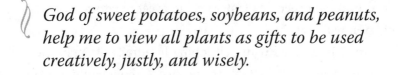

God of sweet potatoes, soybeans, and peanuts, help me to view all plants as gifts to be used creatively, justly, and wisely.

11

Time

What is this life, if full of care
We have no time to stand and stare?

❧ WILLIAM DAVIES

*O*n my way out of the dentist's office, I made an appointment for my next six-month checkup, carefully marking it in the small calendar I keep in my purse: Tuesday, March 15 at 8:50 AM. I had to smile. Making an appointment that far in advance is pretty presumptuous. Who knows where I will be in March or in what condition I will be on that particular day, at that precise time. Why, I do not even know if I will be alive or not! (Often I book my speaking engagements and retreats two years in advance! That must make God smile.)

I was thinking: God is the author of Time, yes, but God never made a clock. God made the mornings, noons, afternoons, evenings, and nights. God never made a calendar either. God made the seasons. It was we humans who took the gift of time and chopped it up into segments: months, weeks, days, hours, minutes, seconds, and nanoseconds. It was we who hung big clocks on our walls and stuck little clocks on our wrists. And how many times a day do we pay homage to the clock gods by glancing at the wall or peeking at our wrist? A friend of mine told me that he stopped wearing a watch two years ago and, although a very busy man, he gets along fine without it. I am not quite so daring.

Measuring time accurately is a rather recent phenomenon. For centuries people lived their lives without knowing what time it was. Then town clocks sprang up in villages and began tolling the time for all the villagers to hear. But even those clocks were notoriously inaccurate. A town clock was considered good even if it was an hour or two off. What a contrast to today's world where we have atomic clocks that reset themselves automatically if they are a fraction of a second off.

Sometimes I wonder if, by chopping time up into little pieces, we have lost touch with the larger movements of time. Ironically, civilizations with the most sophisticated time pieces are sometimes the very ones who have lost track of the larger movements of time—the turning of the leaves, the migratory patterns of birds, the barely perceptible shortening of the days as we move toward fall, the lengthening of shadows during winter. And another thing I wonder about: What is the point of knowing precisely what time of day or night it is if we no longer know what time is for?

That is one reason I love to make a retreat or even a day of recollection. On retreat, I am freed from clocks. I get up not when an alarm goes off, but when I feel like getting up. During retreat I have virtually no appointments except maybe to show up for

Mass or meet with a spiritual director. I eat lunch not when the clock says noon, but when my stomach says, "I'm hungry." I pray not for fifteen minutes or not at 5:00. Instead the whole day becomes a prayer. And I go to bed in the evening when I am too sleepy to stay up any longer.

The spiritual writer Hans Urs Von Balthasar has said some wise things about time. He detects irony in the fact that "We grow only by being thrust into transiency." In addition, "We cannot ripen, we cannot become rich in any way other than by the uninterrupted renunciation that occurs hour by hour." Balthasar encourages us to face time like "a beggar at the gate of the future." Let time "teach you to squander."

Time teaches us to squander. It teaches us to let go of this particular moment in order to embrace the next. Sometimes we also have to let go of our ticking clocks in order to get in touch with the seamless garment of God's time. We have to step out of time, so to speak, to appreciate the gift that it is.

Reflection • Discussion

What is my attitude toward time?

How often do I look at my watch or a clock during the day?

How in touch am I with the larger movements of time seen in nature?

My times are in your hands.   — PSALM 31:16

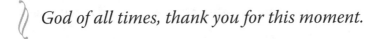 *God of all times, thank you for this moment.*

12

Shining Dawn

*Naught is possessed, neither gold, nor
land, nor love, nor peace, nor even sorrow
nor death, nor yet salvation. Say of
nothing: It is mine. Say only: It is with me.*

☛ D.H. LAWRENCE

ho am I? 1) I have been highly sought after throughout human history because of my beauty and scarcity. 2) I was one of the gifts the three Magi brought to the baby Jesus. 3) I was largely responsible for the European exploration of the Americas. 4) For many years I was the financial standard for international trade. And 5) I am said to line the streets of heaven. If you answered gold, you are right.

Gold is a precious metal with the chemical symbol Au, which stands for *aurum*, Latin for "shining dawn." Gold's unique place in history stems not only from its beauty, but also from its relative scarcity and its unique composition. Let's face it. If gold were as abundant as the sand on the shore or the dandelions in your lawn, it would lose much of its allure. Case in point: In Thomas More's fictional *Utopia*, gold is so abundant on the island that it is used to make toilet seats! But the fact that gold has to be found first (often painstakingly) and then mined (often painstakingly), makes gold extremely valuable. The composition of gold is unique too. First, it is the only yellow metal. (The word "gold" comes from the Old English geolu meaning yellow.) Gold is dense, soft, and the most malleable of known metals. A single ounce of gold can be stretched into a wire five miles long.

Pure gold (24 carat) is too soft for ordinary use, so it is usually hardened by alloying it with copper or other base metals. The gold coins used between 1526 and 1930 were typically 22k. Gold jewelry is usually between 22k and 10k. In medieval times, gold was considered beneficial to health and was actually ingested. The people back them reasoned that anything so rare and beautiful had to be good for one's health. Even today gold salts are used in the treatment of arthritis, whereas gold leaf is put into gourmet drinks and sweets.

Another property gold possesses is its virtual indestructibility. Gold is a "noble" metal which means it does not oxidize (rust or tarnish) under normal conditions. Gold is also an excellent and reliable conductor, and is widely used in circuitry to ensure the reliability of equipment operation—from the deployment of airbags in cars to the deployment of satellites in space.

For many years gold has been used in dentistry as well. More recently, surgeons use gold instruments to clear blocked arteries, and they inject gold pellets to stop the spread of prostate cancer in men. Because of gold's high electrical conductivity, it is a principal component in all kinds of electrical devices including computers. Gold also reflects infrared rays extremely well. When the astronauts landed on the moon in 1969 they were sporting gold-coated visors to protect their eyes from the burning sun.

Gold is beautiful to behold. It is rare and precious. It has also proven itself exceedingly useful for humans. But we must remember: Though gold has been responsible for the rise and fall of whole civilizations, gold is still only gold. It is only one metal among many. As the proverb reminds us: "Don't miss all the beautiful colors of the rainbow looking for that pot of gold."

Reflection • Discussion

Why has gold held such a fascination for so many people throughout history?

What has been the role of gold in my personal life?

What do I think of the introductory quote and the proverb at the end of this chapter?

> "Do not take gold or silver or copper for your belts; no sack for the journey, or a second tunic, or sandals, or walking stick."   — MATTHEW 10:9–10

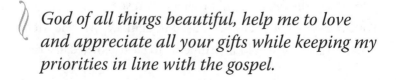

God of all things beautiful, help me to love and appreciate all your gifts while keeping my priorities in line with the gospel.

13

The Bird in My Hands

To see the world in a grain of sand,
and heaven in a wild flower.
Hold infinity in the palm of your hand,
and eternity in an hour.

— WILLIAM BLAKE

I was walking from the school to the convent one spring afternoon when I spotted a tiny, brown bird lying on the sidewalk by the glass doors. At first I thought she was dead. But as I stooped down to get a better look, I saw she was alive. I immediately deduced that she had flown into the glass doors and was injured or at least stunned. How long she had been lying there, I did not know. Feeling the chilly air, I instinctively picked her up in my hands. She made no protest. I sat down on a nearby bench and held her in the warm cave of my cupped hands.

As I sat there, I could feel the bird's heart beating rapidly. I began to marvel at the miracle of it all. Here was I holding a live bird in my hands! I was enough of a realist to know that she could very well die in my hands. But I took hope in the fact that she looked whole. I detected no broken wing, no flopping neck. But who knew what unobservable injuries she might have sustained? The optimist in me wanted to believe she was merely stunned, and soon, benefiting from the warmth of my hands, she would fly away.

Along the bumpy road of life, optimism does not always pay off. But this time it did. After several minutes, I began to feel the tiny bird's gradual stirring in my hands. A few minutes later, I cautiously opened my hands. For one fleeting moment the tiny bird just sat there in the palm of my outstretched hand. The next instant, she flew away.

I thanked God that I had happened by at just the right moment, that I had spotted the bird, and that I could play a small part in her recovery through the warmth of my hands.

Reflection • Discussion

Have I ever had a similar encounter with a bird or animal?

How can I use the warmth of my love to help someone today?

> Do not be afraid. You are worth more than many
> sparrows.   — LUKE 12:7

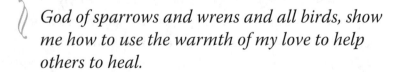

God of sparrows and wrens and all birds, show me how to use the warmth of my love to help others to heal.

14

A Theology of Sleep

Sleep is one of God's moments. A time that refreshes; a time when God counsels and inspires.

➤ VICTOR HOAGLAND, CP

Sleep is the natural periodic suspension of consciousness observed throughout the animal world. All mammals sleep. All birds sleep. Many reptiles, amphibians, and fish sleep. Although sleep has been the subject of intense research, we are just beginning to understand how sleep affects the physical and mental health of beings—especially human beings.

The National Sleep Foundation in the United States says that adult humans need eight to nine hours of sleep per day. (Babies need sixteen to eighteen hours and teenagers nine to ten.) Sleep benefits alertness, memory, problem solving, and overall health. It also reduces the risk of accidents. The National Highway Department reports that sleep deprivation causes 100,000 traffic accidents per year. The catastrophes at the Chernobyl nuclear power plant and with the Exxon Valdez off the coast of Alaska were partly due to sleep deprivation.

Researchers tell us that we, as a nation, are essentially sleep deprived. The average adult gets only six hours and fifty-eight minutes of sleep per day. Many people get a lot less. With the invention of the light bulb, we can keep working long after the sun has set. Some of us think of sleep as a luxury we can't afford, rather than a necessity for our basic survival. We have bought into the maxim, "You snooze, you lose." Ironically, we often cut down on our sleep in the name of productivity, when, in reality, we may be more productive if we slept more.

The French poet Charles Peguy's beautiful poem, "Sleep," links sleep with trust in God. In the poem, God laments the fact that humans aren't getting enough sleep. God says, "…they tell me that there are men / Who work well and sleep badly. / Who don't sleep. What lack of confidence in me." Granted, there can be other causes for sleeplessness besides lack of trust in God. Drugs, alcohol, or physical conditions such as apnea can interfere with sleep. But many of us have to admit that often it is our fears and anxieties that keep us tossing and turning at night.

Scripture offers us a unique perspective on sleep. In Genesis, for example, when God is creating the universe, God rests between each day. On the seventh day, God rests the entire day (Gn 1—2:4). The implication is that rest (or sleep) is an essential component of God's creativity, a creativity we share in as God's sons and daughters. Psalm 127 connects sleep with trust in God: "It is vain for you to rise early / and put off your rest at night; / To eat bread earned by hard toil— / all this God gives to his beloved in sleep" (Ps 127:2). In addition, Scripture shows God communicating to individuals while they sleep—most notably Jacob, the prophet Samuel, and St. Joseph.

Jesus slept. He slept soundly. We know this, because once, after a long day of preaching and healing, he fell asleep in a boat. A violent storm arose. It was so awful, his friends, some of them seasoned fishermen, feared for their lives. But Jesus would have slept right through if they hadn't awakened him (Mk 4:35–41). On the other hand, Jesus also experienced sleeplessness. In Gethsemane, the night before he died, he was so disturbed by the knowledge of his imminent death that he could not sleep (Mk 14:32–47).

Is there such a thing as "a theology of sleep"? Perhaps. First, when we go to sleep, we are acknowledging our limitations. We are letting go of control. We are reminding ourselves that we are mere creatures, not the creator. Sleep, then, can be one way we consciously hand over all our worries and concerns to God each night. Second, sleep is theological because it has social implications. We can choose to get enough sleep because it helps make us better parents, family members, friends, neighbors, and co-workers. Third, sleep reminds us of values beyond the work that we do. In her article, "Sleep Therapy: In Search of a Counterculture for the Common Good," Lauren Winner writes, "a countercultural embrace of sleep bears witness to values higher than 'the cares of the world, the deceitfulness of riches, and the desire for other things.'"

Reflection • Discussion

How much sleep do I get each day?

What, if anything, interferes with my sleep?

Do I think there is a theology of sleep? Why or why not?

> In peace I shall both lie down and sleep,
> for you alone, Lord, make me secure.   — PSALM 4:8

Watchful God, may I fall asleep tonight and every night, entrusting myself and our world to you.

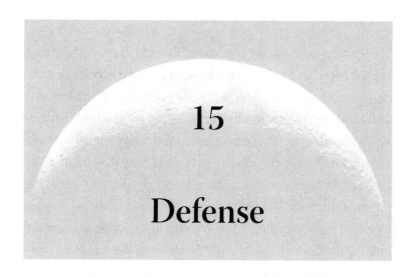

15

Defense

Sometimes we judge someone as mean or cold when, in reality, they are hurting or afraid.

☛ MELANNIE SVOBODA, SND

*I*f you watch any American football game, sooner or later you will hear the crowd yell, "Defense! Defense!" Every football player knows it is not enough for a team to score points, they must also prevent the opposing team from scoring points. They must guard their end zone and do whatever it takes (as long as it is legal) to stop an opposing team member from getting in with the ball. That is defense. Good defense wins football games.

Good defense also preserves lives—at least in the natural world. It is as if the Creator gave every living thing—be it a cactus, moth, jellyfish, chameleon, zebra, elephant, or human—some method of defending itself against predators. Take the cactus. Many cacti (like the Mexican Lime Cactus) have long, sharp needles that discourage animals from taking a big bite out of them. The Emperor Gum Moth (like many moths) has coloring on its wings that look like two huge eyes. These fake eyes scare away many potential predators such as birds. Jellyfish have their sting to ward off predators. If you have ever been stung by a jellyfish, you know it is best to leave them well enough alone. Chameleons can change colors to blend into their background, thus making it more difficult for predators to see them. Chameleons like to taunt, "Now I'm brown, now I'm green. Now by you, I can't be seen!"

Zebras come dressed in those classy black and white stripes which are part of their defense. When zebras clump together in a bunch, those stripes play a trick on the eyes of their predators. It is like seeing a guy on TV with a loud striped shirt. The stripes do crazy things to your eyes. Same principle. For some animals, sheer size is their defense. No one tangles with an adult elephant.

And what about us humans? What defense do we have against predators? In some ways, we are sadly lacking in defense. In size, we are pretty puny next to a moose or a grizzly. We cannot run very fast either. Even crocodiles and emus can outrun us. We cannot change color like the chameleon, although we have learned to don camouflage while hunting or engaging in war. Humans have no stingers, needles, horns, tusks, or venom to speak of. So what is our defense? It is largely our brain, of course. Although we are sorely lacking in defensive measures physically (although we can punch, kick, scream, scratch, and bite), God blessed us with a huge brain that allows us to figure out clever ways to avoid trouble or to escape it.

Knowing about the defensive techniques of plants and animals can actually help us in our dealings with humans. If someone screams at us, for example, we can be more understanding if we realize their scream might really be a part of their defensive posture. We can ask, "Does she feel threatened by me?" or "What is he protecting?" We can also postpone dialogue if the other party is in a purely defensive mode. Little real dialogue can occur once claws are out and teeth are bared.

Reflection • Discussion

What are some other ways plants and animals defend themselves?

What are some of the ways I defend myself when I feel attacked or frightened?

The Lord is my defense.   —PSALM 94:22

God, help me to remember that you alone are my strong defense.

16

The Humble Opposable Thumb

Most human beings have an almost infinite capacity for taking things for granted.

⟶ ALDOUS HUXLEY

*B*efore you read this chapter, do me a favor. Look at your thumb. Either one will do. But do more than merely look at it. Behold your thumb. Gaze at it as if you were seeing your thumb for the first time. Don't rush. Take your time. What do you see? You see a digit that is rather humble in appearance. Compared to the other four fingers on your hand, your thumb is short and stubby. It looks like a finger that forgot to grow. Notice that your thumb has only one joint, too, whereas your other fingers have two. Having only one joint restricts the thumb's movement. To demonstrate this, flex your other four fingers. Now flex your thumb. See what I mean? The thumb is simply less dexterous. It is set apart from the other fingers, too, living its life off to the side of the mainland hand. It reminds me of the kid in the school lunchroom who sits at the same table with the other kids, but is never quite part of the group.

Despite its lowly appearance, despite its disconnection from the other fingers, the thumb is extremely important. In fact, anthropologists tell us the thumb played a critical role in the development of the human species. How? The human thumb (and the thumb of certain other primates such as orangutans and gorillas) is opposable. This means it can face—oppose—the other four fingers. If your hand is healthy, the tip of your thumb can touch the tips of the other four fingers on the same hand. Do that now. See? This neat little trick made it possible for human beings to grasp things. And grasping enabled early humans to make tools, which some claim, is the foundation of human civilization. Today our unassuming thumb helps us to do a wide variety of tasks we may take for granted. It enables us to grab a glass of water, hold a cup of tea, sign our name, play a guitar, catch and throw a baseball, swing a golf club, hold a book to read, fashion clay pots, strike the space bar on a keyboard, and (one of its newest designated tasks) send text messages to our friends.

The thumb has other powers too. In ancient Rome, the gladiators and other unfortunate individuals who found themselves in the center of the sports arena, were keenly aware of the power of the emperor's thumb. Some scholars believe that if the emperor held his thumb up, their lives were spared. If he thrust his thumb down, they were killed. Other scholars think the thumb signals were reversed: up meant kill; down meant live. Either way, that's a lot of power for such a scrubby little digit.

The power of the thumb is shown in other ways too. It is sometimes used as part of obscene gestures. In some cultures, the thumbs up sign is of itself an obscene gesture. It is helpful when you travel internationally to familiarize yourself with another country's gestures to avoid embarrassment. Once I was working with an international group of sisters. To show my agreement with another sister, I flashed her the "okay" sign—at least it meant "okay" in my culture. I brought the tip of my thumb to the tip of my index finger and formed a circle. When she saw my sign, she got this horrified look on her face. Only later did I learn that in her country, my innocent "okay" sign meant something very, very different!

Many human children draw comfort from sucking their thumbs. Thumb sucking can start in the womb as early as fifteen weeks after gestation. Then there's the sport called thumb wrestling in which two opponents lock the four fingers of their right or left hand together and try to pin each other's thumb down for five seconds.

In the English language we have many expressions involving the thumb. The phrase "rule of thumb," for example, originated from English common law which forbad a husband to beat his wife with a stick thicker than his thumb. Every hitchhiker knows how to "thumb a ride." If someone exerts too much control over us, we say they have us "under their thumb," whereas if someone is good with plants, we say they have "a green thumb." To show our contempt for someone, we "thumb our nose" at them, while if we feel out of place, we say we "stick out like a sore thumb." And if we're bored, we can always sit and "twiddle our thumbs."

Reflection • Discussion

Is there anything in this chapter that surprised me? If so, what?

Do I value the work of my thumbs or do I take them for granted?

> Then [Jesus] said to the man, "Stretch out your hand."
> He stretched it out, and it was restored as sound as the
> other.   — MATTHEW 12:13

Ingenious Creator, I thank you for my hands today—and especially for my humble opposable thumbs.

17

Orca the Whale

Whales have had their most advanced brains for almost thirty million years. Our species has existed for about one-thousandth of that time. We have a lot to learn from whales.

⤙ ROGER PAYNE

n William Shakespeare's play *Romeo and Juliet*, Juliet poses the question, "What's in a name? That which we call a rose / By any other name would smell as sweet." Unfortunately, when we look at the names given to the magnificent black-and-white whale often found in aquariums and marine parks, we must admit: there is much in those names that is not very sweet. We call this majestic creature *orcinus orca*, orca, or killer whale. All three names are essentially derogatory. The word *orcinus*, for example, means "from hell." The name orca, since it refers to the

Market Place Mall
20 44 #

When the Moon Slips
Away

$ 6.⁻

Roman god of the underworld, also has shady overtones. And when we call this great whale a "killer whale," we are unjustly investing it with criminal intent. Although all three names do a disservice to this stunning animal, I will use the name orca since it seems the least offensive.

In his beautiful book, *Orca*, Peter Knudtson asks, "Why are we humans so fascinated by whales?" He suggests this answer: "What we are increasingly drawn to may be the fleeting glimpse of a wild beast possessed of such astonishing grace, intelligence and power that it makes us realize, if only for an instant, that we are mere participants in the natural world, not its masters." Orcas humble us. They put us in our place.

They do this, first of all, by their sheer size. Adult male orcas are, on average, thirty feet long and can weigh as much as 17,600 pounds. Females are "only" about eighteen to twenty-three feet long and tip the scales at 5,550 to 8,800 pounds. Another cause of fascination is the fact that these great whales spend ninety-five percent of their time under water, so, although they have been around for millions of years, we know scarcely anything about them.

Perhaps orcas also intrigue us because we have much in common with them. Like us, orcas are mammals. They are warm-blooded, have hair (although a lot less than we do—and none as adults), breathe air into their lungs, give birth to and nurse their young. In addition, orcas enjoy a wide geographic distribution. They are found in every major ocean and sea on earth, from the frigid waters of the arctic to the warm waters of the tropics. The only other mammal that has a wider geographic distribution is homo sapiens.

Orcas possess a spectacular array of gifts. Their sleek torpedo-like shape enables them to swim gracefully and fast with speeds up to thirty-five miles per hour. With their built-in biosonar system they use sound to "see" their surroundings. They also possess remarkable intelligence. Classical animal IQ tests rate orcas' mental capabilities somewhere between those of dogs and chimpanzees. In addition, orcas are highly vocal, producing a variety of calls, clicks, and whistles. They communicate with each other constantly, sometimes over vast distances—up to ten miles. Scientists believe each pod or group of whales has a unique dialect. Mother orcas have been observed teaching their calves the pod's dialect.

The breathing of these whales is also intriguing. Their nostrils (or blowholes) are not located on the tip of their snout like so many fish and other animals, but rather on the top of their heads. This enables them to breathe while still being partially submerged in water. The blowhole also separates breathing from eating. Orcas won't choke on their food the way we humans sometimes do when we try to talk and eat at the same time. And one more interesting fact about their breathing: the highly social orcas practice synchronized breathing within their pod. This communal respiration probably serves as a display of family unity or even affection.

How did these beautiful animals get such a bad reputation for murder and mayhem? For one thing, orcas sit at the top of the marine food chain. Having no natural predators, they can rightfully boast, "We're number one!" This fact alone is enough to cause some people to hate orcas—much as some people (myself included) hate the New York Yankees. Such loathing, though understandable, is not completely rational.

But orcas are no more malicious than the robin pecking for worms on your front lawn. Since they are so huge, however, they need to eat a lot more than a few worms each day. In fact orcas need about 500 pounds of food (fish, seals, sea lions, and even other whales) each day to survive and stay healthy. Unfortunately, their simple need for food can look like rapacity and malice.

So what should be our attitude to orca? Perhaps the American artist and whale expert Richard Ellis says it best: Orca "is not an unreconstructed murderer; neither is it a jolly circus clown, to be made to jump through hoops for entertainment. The real orca lies somewhere between these two extremes; or maybe we will find that it is beyond the shape of our understanding."

Reflection • Discussion

What intrigues me the most about orcas?

Do I think orcas should be kept in captivity? Why or why not?

Have I ever gone whale watching? Would I like to? Why or why not?

But the Lord sent a large fish, that swallowed Jonah; and he remained in the belly of the fish for three days and three nights.   — JONAH 2:1

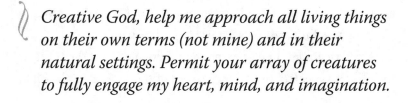

Creative God, help me approach all living things on their own terms (not mine) and in their natural settings. Permit your array of creatures to fully engage my heart, mind, and imagination.

18

The Tulip Catalogue

We should bow down before the orchid and the snail and join our palms reverently before the monarch butterfly and the magnolia tree. The feeling of respect for all species will help us recognize the noblest nature in ourselves.

☞ THICH NHAT HANH

A number of years ago I was leafing through one of my father's seed catalogues and was struck by the beautiful colored pictures of various plants and flowers. Thinking I might use them to make some homemade cards someday, I asked my father if he would save me a few of his seed catalogues when he was finished with them. He said he would.

A few weeks later he gave me the catalogues—not the three or four I had expected, but twenty-seven of them! That night I had an inspiration. Instead of reading my novel in bed before falling asleep, I decided to read a seed catalogue. I randomly selected one of them. It happened to be a catalogue devoted entirely to tulips—almost forty pages worth.

As I slowly paged through the catalogue, gazing at one tulip after another, something marvelous happened. I found myself totally captivated by tulips—their color, their shape, their variation, their mystery, their names. Until then I had assumed I knew something about tulips. I knew, for example, that they grew from bulbs, they bloomed in early spring, and they came in several colors like red, yellow, and white. Simple. But the tulip catalogue said to me, "No, not so simple!" It welcomed me into the real world of tulips where I learned many new things.

I learned there are many varieties of tulips. They come in a wide range of colors including pure white, vivid green, deep red, flaming orange, and even dark purple. Some tulips are solid in color; others are striped, spotted, or splashed with several different colors. Some tulips are short and stocky; others are tall and lean. Most have blossoms with smooth edges, but a few varieties come with fringed edges. Some tulips are tiny, while others are jumbo-sized—with one bloom measuring ten inches across! The copyrighted names of the tulips also intrigued me, names like yellow emperor, burgundy lace, flaming parrot, Arabian mystery, and dorie overall.

After about twenty minutes of "reading" the tulip catalogue, I felt very refreshed—and somehow closer to God. I couldn't help thinking: if tulips are so filled with beauty and mystery, how much more must be the person who created them? As I put my tulip catalogue away, I couldn't stop myself from peeking at the other catalogues. They were devoted to irises, berries, trees, shrubs, apples, vegetables, and American Beauty Roses. I knew I had many more evenings of good reading (and good praying) ahead of me!

Reflection • Discussion

Have I ever browsed through a seed or flower catalogue? If so, what were some of my thoughts and feelings as I did?

What flower, fruit, or vegetable of God's creation especially impresses or intrigues me? Why?

> Then the Lord God planted a garden in Eden, in the
> east, and he placed there the man whom he had formed.
> Out of the ground the Lord God made various trees
> grow that were delightful to look at.   — GENESIS 2:8–9

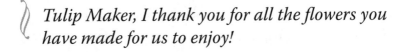 *Tulip Maker, I thank you for all the flowers you have made for us to enjoy!*

19

The Magic of Flight

Flying was a very tangible freedom.
In those days, it was beauty, adventure,
discovery—the epitome of breaking into
new worlds.

☙ ANNE MORROW LINDBERGH

*T*hroughout history, human beings have been fascinated
with flight. When the earliest people gazed up into the
sky and beheld the birds soaring high above them, they
probably said, "I wish I could do that!" But it wasn't until thousands of year later (the year 1783 to be exact) when the Montgolfier
brothers successfully flew their first untethered hot air balloon over
the French countryside, that people could finally say, "We can fly!"
Since that historic day, we have made remarkable strides in avia-
tion—from the Wright brothers' primitive plane at Kitty Hawk to
our present-day gliders, helicopters, jet airplanes, and spacecraft.

Writing for *Smithsonian* magazine, Michael Parfit raises this question: "Can the magic of flight ever be carried by words?" His answer: "I think not." I agree with him. Despite that fact, though, I will attempt to capture three aspects of the magic of flight in these few words.

First, there is magic in the flight of certain members of the animal world, most notably the insects, birds, and bats. Yes, there are flying frogs, flying lizards, and flying snakes, but their gliding can't begin to compare with the maneuverability and grace of the Blue-eyed Darner Dragonfly, the California condor, or the Mexican Funnel-eared Bat. The fastest flyer in the animal world is the Peregrine falcon which, in a dive, can exceed 199 miles per hour. The hummingbird, whose tiny wings beat 90 times per second, can do something no other bird can do: fly backwards and upside down. Bats are stellar flyers too, which is all the more remarkable since they are blind. Bats use their built-in sonar system to avoid crashing into trees, barns, and such, and to locate their prey.

There is magic also in the basic physics of mechanical flight. Mechanical flight is made possible by the interaction of four forces: 1) weight—the down force caused by gravity, 2) lift—the up force caused by air moving over the wings, 3) drag—the backward force caused by air resistance, and 4) thrust—the forward force caused by the engine. Simply put, lift overcomes the force of gravity for takeoff, but gravity overcomes the force of lift for landing. Similarly, thrust overcomes the force of drag for forward movement, while drag overcomes the force of thrust for stopping. It is by utilizing the natural tension among these four forces that a plane is able to take off, fly, and land successfully. Knowledge of this fact helps me to view the various tensions in my own life in a more positive vein. I ask myself, how well do I understand the various forces at work in my life right now, and how well am I able to utilize these forces for some good or advantage?

Third, flight is magic because it has had a profound psychological and cultural impact upon humanity. French writer and pilot Antoine de Saint-Exupéry wrote, "I fly because it releases my mind from the tyranny of petty things." Decades later astronaut Roger Chaffee echoed similar sentiments when he said, "Problems look mighty small from 150 miles up." Flight, then, can give us a wider perspective on life. In addition, flight has given us a wonderful metaphor for life. Shortly before Charles Lindbergh took off from New York on his historic solo flight to Paris, he reflected on the apparent folly of his endeavor, a folly that included trusting in the air—the thin air which he could not see—to hold him up during his trek across the Atlantic. One metaphor that flight has given us is this: sometimes we must learn to trust in what we cannot see. At times, God falls into that category!

Flight also has had a significant cultural impact on humanity. Writer Wendell Wilkie said, "The modern airplane creates a new geographic dimension...the world is small, the world is one." Perhaps no single photograph has captured this better than the photograph of planet earth taken by the Apollo 17 crew on their way to the moon. That picture of our blue and white planet suspended against the utter blackness of outer space truly captured the smallness, beauty, and oneness of the planet we all call home. Bill Gates, CEO of Microsoft Corporation, credited flight with yet another magic when he said, "The Wright brothers created the single greatest cultural force since the invention of writing.

The airplane became the first World Wide Web, bringing people, languages, ideas, and values together."

John Gillespie Magee, both poet and pilot, wrote the sonnet "High Flight" shortly before he died at age 19 in a military training exercise in 1942. The poem has always been for me the classic expression of flight. Its often-quoted opening and closing lines are these:

"Oh! I have slipped the surly bonds of earth….Put out my hand and touched the face of God."

Reflection • Discussion

What is my attitude toward flying? Why?

What things help to "release my mind from the tyranny of petty things"?

What are some of the natural forces or tensions in my life that I can work with for some good or advantage?

They that hope in the Lord will renew their strength,
they will soar as with eagles' wings.　　— ISAIAH 40:31

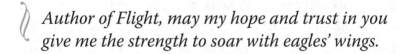 *Author of Flight, may my hope and trust in you give me the strength to soar with eagles' wings.*

20

The Grand, Grand Canyon

The shudder of awe is humanity's highest faculty.

☙ GOETHE

*I*n the winter of 1857-58, Lt. Joseph Christmas Ives of the Corp of Topographical Engineers of the U.S. Army was commissioned to lead an expedition down the Colorado River in Arizona to ascertain its navigability. He and his men were probably only the third group of white men to actually see the Grand Canyon. In his report, Ives wrote the following: "It (the Grand Canyon) looks like the Gates of Hell. The region is, of course, altogether valueless. It can be approached only from the south, and after entering it, there is nothing to do but leave." He concluded that the Grand Canyon "seems intended by nature [to be] forever unvisited and undisturbed."

It is hard to comprehend how Ives and his party missed seeing the Grand Canyon for what is really is: a natural wonder which, in the words of Theodore Roosevelt, is "absolutely unparalleled throughout the rest of the world." And what would Ives and his companions think of the five million people each year who flock to the Grand Canyon—a place he thought would be "forever unvisited"? (In fairness to Ives, we must remember that he was scoping out the area for military and strategic purposes. As such, the Grand Canyon had little use.)

I have never been to the Grand Canyon. I have only seen it in pictures and movies and read about it in books. I have only heard visitors to the Grand Canyon describe their experience with wonder and awe in their voices. One of my friends said when she saw it for the first time, she actually wept for the sheer beauty of the place. Evidently, many people share that experience. Though the magnificence of the Grand Canyon cannot be captured in words, I nonetheless offer these few paragraphs on this breathtaking natural wonder.

The Grand Canyon can be defined as a colorful, steep-sided gorge carved out by the Colorado River in the state of Arizona. Those who have seen the Grand Canyon, however, know how inadequate such a definition is. Perhaps a few statistics might help to give us a greater appreciation of this "steep-sided gorge." The Grand Canyon is big. It is 277 miles long. The Grand Canyon is wide—anywhere from .25 to 15 miles across. And it is deep—more than a mile in some places. If you put the mighty Niagara Falls into the Grand Canyon or the tallest skyscraper in the world, they would be dwarfed by the immensity of this gorge. Though the Grand Canyon is not the deepest canyon in the world, it is the most spectacular due largely to its massive size and colorful landscape. Depending on the sun, the colors of the walls of the canyon can be red, orange, yellow, blue, magenta, pink, lavender, brown, gray, and even black. The Grand Canyon is also very old. Some scientists say it was formed about five to six million years ago; others say seventeen million years ago.

What factors contributed to the formation of the Grand Canyon as we know it today? Geologists cite several factors: the continental shift (the Grand Canyon used to be farther south) ancient seas (several times it was covered by oceans), volcanic activity (this occurred about one billion years ago), and the Colorado River itself. But by and large most of the splendor of the Grand Canyon was caused by simple erosion—especially by water (ice) and wind. Henry David Thoreau said this about the persistent power of erosion: "The finest workers in stone are not copper or steel tools, but the gentle touches of air and water working at their leisure with a liberal allowance of time." Two things strike me about the formation of the Grand Canyon. First, its formation proves that persistent gentleness coupled with a liberal allowance of time can bring about something wonderful. And second, it was subtraction and not addition that brought about the beauty of the Grand Canyon. I think there's a lesson for the spiritual life in both of those facts.

Another amazing fact about the Grand Canyon is this: two billion years of the history of the earth is exposed in its canyon walls. Over millions of years the Colorado River and its tributaries cut through layer after layer of rock, revealing the earth's history. As someone has aptly said, "Looking at the Grand Canyon is like looking at the pages from a history book."

The people who operate Grand Canyon National Park realize that people come to see the Grand Canyon not merely because it is so big and colorful. They come for more intangible reasons. These are the words from one of the Grand Canyon National Park brochures: "This canyon is a gift that transcends what we experience. Its beauty and size humbles us. Its timelessness provokes a comparison to our short existence. In its vast spaces we find solace from our hectic lives."

In our sophisticated and busy world, not many things can stun people into silence by their massiveness, nor bring tears to people's eyes by their sheer loveliness. But the Grand Canyon does exactly that to people. The Grand Canyon is, indeed, grand.

Reflection • Discussion

If I have been to the Grand Canyon, what was my response?

If I have not been there, are there other natural wonders I have experienced that have stunned me into silence or brought tears to my eyes?

Have I ever experienced "persistent gentleness" or "erosion" in a positive way in my life?

Majestic and glorious is your work,
your wise design endures forever." — PSALM 111:3

I thank you, God, for the Grand Canyon and for all the natural wonders of the earth.

21

"I Let the Turtle Go"

*Something in me chills at the thought of
keeping a box turtle for a pet, of putting a
creature that may be as old as my mother
into a cardboard box...[just] for the
pleasure of having it.*

          JULIE ZICKEFOOSE

*I*was novice director for my community in the 1980s. At one
point, the novice directors and novices in the Cleveland
area used to meet several times a year at one of the mother-
houses located in a beautiful rural area. In between conferences,
talks, and prayer, the novices had the chance to relax with each
other and to enjoy the spacious grounds, which included lawns,
meadows, woods, and a couple of lakes.

One late afternoon, one of my novices, Sister Debra, came
running to me excitedly carrying a small turtle in her hands. I

could tell by its dome-shaped shell and its markings that it was a box turtle. Deb was fascinated by the creature and told me she was going to take it home with us the next day and maybe keep it as a pet. Needless to say, I was not at all enthusiastic about her plans. Where would she keep it? What would we feed it? And how did the poor turtle feel about the prospect of being transported 40 miles from its home? Yet I didn't want to jump the gun and say, "No, you put that turtle back! We are not taking it home with us!" So I didn't openly object to her plans. But inwardly I prayed, "Dear God, please bring her to change her mind!"

I went to bed that night worrying about the novice—and the turtle. But when I got up the next morning, there was a note under my door. Written in Deb's distinctive handwriting were these simple words: "I let the turtle go." I breathed a sign of relief. I thanked God that she had made a good decision—the right decision—and that she had made it on her own.

The more I read about box turtles the more I am convinced that they shouldn't be kept as pets—for many reasons. First, the turtles need to roam outdoors. You cannot keep a box turtle in a confined space without causing it considerable stress. Second, these turtles should not be handled, so they don't make good pets for children or adults who often want a pet to cuddle and play with. Third, box turtles need variety in their diet. They eat different food at different times in their life. From one to five years they're basically carnivores. This means they need to eat snails, insects, slugs, worms, birds, and small rodents. But as adults, they're herbivores, except they do not eat green leaves.

A fourth reason these turtles shouldn't be kept as pets is the fact that their droppings are filled with samonella, which is harmless for them, but can be harmful for humans. Fifth, these turtles live a long time—forty years or even longer. How many people are willing to make a forty-year commitment to a pet? Sixth, box turtles are susceptible to various kinds of infections. Hence, they often need the care of a reptile vet. And last, box turtles are "homebodies." They desire to live and breed wherever they happen to be born. If you take a box turtle even only a mile from where you found it, it will spend years pining and searching for its original home.

Because of the popularity of turtles for pets, box turtles are routinely captured in this country and sold here and abroad— especially in Europe. In one forty-one month period alone, for example, nearly 30,000 of these turtles in Louisiana were taken from the wild for resale. Needless to say, such actions are having a grave detrimental effect on the box turtle population in this country.

In her book, *Letters from Eden*, Julie Zickefoose devotes a chapter to box turtles. She writes that she struggles "to reconcile humanity's appalling treatment of this ancient creature with common sense and prudence. For me it all comes down to a simple issue: respect. Respect, distinct from love, for we can love a species to death."

Reflection • Discussion

What has been my experience with turtles? with other pets?

Do I agree with Zickefoose that respect is distinct from love?

Have I ever loved something to death?

Love is patient, love is kind…it does not seek its own interests…but rejoices with the truth.

— 1 CORINTHIANS 13:4–6

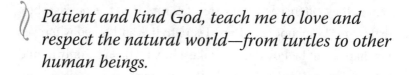 *Patient and kind God, teach me to love and respect the natural world—from turtles to other human beings.*

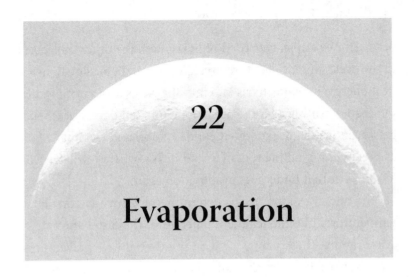

22

Evaporation

*All around us water is rising / on invisible
wings.*

JOHN UPDIKE

You throw a load of wet clothes into the dryer. Forty minutes later, they're dry. Where did the water go? You go for a jog in the park on a warm day. Immediately you begin to perspire. Why? You pour yourself a glass of fresh water. How old is that water in your glass?

The topic of this chapter is evaporation. That may sound like a pretty dull subject, but I hope to show how amazing this process really is and how important it is for life on earth. Along the way, I will answer the questions posed in the previous paragraph.

The water on earth moves in a continuous cycle: evaporation, condensation, and precipitation. Evaporation is the process that turns a liquid to vapor. When a single molecule of water in the

73

ocean, for example, gets tired of living with the other molecules in the ocean, it may decide to break free from them. Slowly, using heat energy, it begins to rise up into the air as a vapor molecule. Off it goes drifting over the ocean for about ten days. But when it gets over Seattle, it undergoes condensation and eventually falls as precipitation on the roof of a Starbucks—where it will sit for a few days until it undergoes evaporation again.

The rate of evaporation is determined by three factors. First, temperature. The higher the temperature, the faster the rate of evaporation. That's why your grandmother always prayed for a nice, warm day when she hung her clothes on the line to dry. Second, wind. Your grandmother also prayed for a nice breeze on laundry day. And third, humidity. The lower the humidity, the faster the evaporation. On a very humid day, your grandmother used to moan, "These clothes will never dry!"

Evaporation from oceans, seas, and lakes accounts for ninety percent of the water delivered as precipitation to the earth. The other ten percent comes from plants. The incredible thing is that water is used over and over again. This means the water you drink today may be the same water that was drunk by a dinosaur or even Jesus!

We use evaporation to control our body temperature too. Runners generate heat when they run. This heat can be life-threatening unless it is transferred from their bodies to the surrounding environment. That's where evaporation comes in. Runners perspire. The water secretions (sweat) absorb body heat and carry this heat from inside the body out into the environment. Simply put, without evaporation, there would be no joggers.

Evaporation is used in other ways too. Most of the world's salt is produced within huge evaporating ponds, a technique employed by people for thousands of years. Other minerals in water, such as magnesium, potash, and bromine, are produced through evaporation. One industrial application of evaporation is to separate crude petroleum into gasoline, kerosene, and gas oil.

The poet John Updike has written an ode to evaporation in his book *Facing Nature*. In the poem, he praises evaporation for its "Fidelity of process!" He notes that housewives trust this "faithful process" to dry their clothes, just as the people on Anguilla trust evaporation for their annual harvest of salt. His poem raises this question for me: what other "faithful processes" do I trust (perhaps unmindfully) in my everyday life?

Reflection • Discussion

What role does evaporation play in my life?

Is there anything in this chapter that particularly struck me? Why?

What other "faithful processes" do I trust in my everyday life?

> Lo, God is great beyond our knowledge;
> the number of his years is past searching out.
> He holds in check the waterdrops that
> filter in rain through his mists,
> Till the skies run with them
> and the showers rain down on mankind.
>
> — JOB 36:26–28

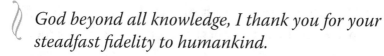

God beyond all knowledge, I thank you for your steadfast fidelity to humankind.

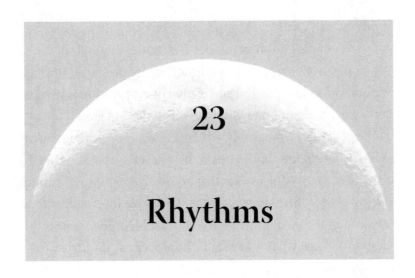

23

Rhythms

Fun is a better way to run a planet.

☞ STATEMENT FROM THE
RHYTHM SOCIETY

One day Thomas Merton, the Trappist monk and writer, sat in his hermitage in the Kentucky woods and listened to the rain pounding down on the roof of his cabin "with insistent and controlled rhythms." He wrote, "And I listen because it reminds me again and again that the whole world turns by rhythms I have not yet learned to recognize, rhythms that are not those of the engineer."

Rain is one obvious rhythm in nature. There are many others. Philosopher Alan Watts said, "Rhythm lies at the heart of play, and these various rhythmic actions are the primordial forms of delight." Nature is replete with rhythms that bring delight: the song of a wren, the chirping of crickets, the movement of the sun across the sky, the waxing and waning of the moon, the beating of the heart, the turning of the seasons, the howling of the wind, the chatter of a brook. There are also rhythms we humans have created: the ticking of a clock, the hum of a refrigerator, the beat of a catchy song, the cadence of a favorite poem, and the flow of a finely crafted sentence.

Then there's the rhythm of dance. In his book *Quantum Theology: Spiritual Implications of the New Physics*, Diarmuid O'Murchu writes this about dance: "In its origin and evolution, dance is fundamentally spiritual and its primary innate function is to facilitate contact with the sacred and divine." This link between dance and worship is seen in Scripture. When the Israelites successfully crossed the Red Sea, they danced with joy: "The Prophetess Miriam, Aaron's sister, took a tambourine in her hand, while all the women went out after her with tambourines, dancing; and she led them in the refrain: Sing to the Lord, for he is gloriously triumphant" (Ex 15:20–21). When the Ark of the Covenant was brought to the city of David, it was greeted with song and dance. King David himself led the dance: "Then David, girt with a linen apron, came dancing before the Lord with abandon" (2 Sam 6:14).

With abandon. I like that. Whether we are dancing the polka, beating a set of bongo drums, or singing with deep passion a favorite song, we naturally give ourselves over to the rhythm—with abandon. There is, in the words of Alan Watts, "the ecstatic loss of self" at such moments, a blending of ourselves with cadences beyond ourselves. At such times we are one with rhythms we cannot name.

I believe the more we are in sync with the many natural rhythms that surround us and reside within us, the happier we are. And conversely, the more we ignore these rhythms or go against them, the more miserable we make ourselves.

Reflection • Discussion

What are some of the natural rhythms around and within me that I am in sync with?

Are there any that I am ignoring or going against?

What role should dance have in contemporary worship?

> There is an appointed time for everything,
> and a time for every affair under the heavens.
>
> — ECCLESIASTES 3:1

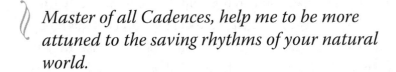 *Master of all Cadences, help me to be more attuned to the saving rhythms of your natural world.*

24

The Look of a Look

I have nothing to offer except a way of looking at things.

☞ ERIK ERIKSON

They say if you happen to run into a grizzly bear while you're hiking in the woods, one thing you should not do is look him (or her) in the eye. Eye contact in the world of animals is often interpreted as aggression.

I experienced this aggression firsthand one day when I was visiting my sister. I experienced it not in my sister, but in her cat Chloe. Chloe is a long-haired, black and white cat with a touch of butterscotch. She tends to be extremely shy when it comes to meeting people. When company comes over, Chloe dashes under the bed and does not emerge again until all the guests are gone. Over the years, I felt Chloe was warming up to me and responding well to my efforts to befriend her. Gradually she began staying in the living room when I came over. Then she began to rub my legs. Eventually she crawled up into my lap and even permitted me the inestimable privilege of petting her. I thought our friendship was sealed.

But one day, while my sister was at work, I was writing on her kitchen table. Chloe was sitting on the table, a foot or so away from my notebook, seemingly content. It could have been a scene from a Norman Rockwell painting. There we were, human and cat, in perfect harmony. But then I paused from my writing and looked up, directly into Chloe's yellow eyes. I did not say anything, I did not make any sudden move, I just looked at her—rather fondly, I thought. Instantly, she growled, hissed at me, jumped off the table, and shot out of the room. I was shocked! What had I done to cause such a conniption? I had just looked at her. Then I remembered that thing I had read about animals and eye contact. I concluded that Chloe had interpreted my gaze of affection as a glare of aggression.

There is a power in looking directly into the eyes of another. Sometimes the look may be a sign of aggression. Just watch the way professional wrestlers glower at their opponents in the ring. Or remember how bothered you were as a kid when your sibling would annoy you by staring at you? "Mommy, tell Johnny to stop looking at me!" But a look can also be a sign of affection, respect, or admiration. We humans instinctively stare at people we find attractive or fascinating. Look at the way the teenage boy sneaks a peek at the pretty girl walking by, the way the young couple ogle at each other across the café table, or the way a young father gazes down upon his sleeping newborn son.

A look can say, "I hate you! You're ugly! Stay away!" But a look can also say: "I like you. I think you're beautiful. Come closer!" As my incident with Chloe the cat reminded me, there is tremendous power in the look of a look.

Reflection • Discussion

Has anyone every misinterpreted a look I gave them?

Do I ever give looks of aggression?

Do I ever give looks of love and respect?

But as for me, I will look to the Lord,
I will put my trust in God my savior.   — MICAH 7:7

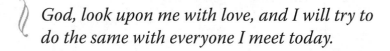

God, look upon me with love, and I will try to do the same with everyone I meet today.

25

Mud

The farthest star and the mud at my feet
are a family; and there is no decency
or sense in honoring one thing, or a few
things, and then closing the list.

☞ MARY OLIVER

As a little girl, I had a fondness for mud. We always seemed to have plenty of it on the farm. The edges of our pond were usually muddy and embedded with the webbed footprints of our geese. The small corral behind the big brown barn was mostly mud where the previous owners had kept a few cows. There was mud between the rows of plants in the garden and even in the low spots in the driveway when it rained. I can remember getting stuck in the mud once when I was about four. I cried and cried until my mother had to come and pull me out.

I also remember playing with mud. Although I do not recall ever making mud pies, I do remember making mud soup with my girlfriend, G-G. Of course, we made up the recipe as we went along: water, grass, stones, a few twigs, and several chunks of nice brown mud. Gradually my fondness for mud turned to disgust. When, how, and why this happened, I am not sure. But as I evolved into a young lady, I assumed a distasteful attitude toward mud best summarized by the word, "Yuck!" I began to think that mud was worthless. Only later did I regain respect for mud.

Mud is defined as a semi-liquid mixture of water and some combination of silt, soil, or clay. Mud is not the same as muck, sometimes called "black soil," which contains more humus and less sand than mud. Muck is found mainly when wetlands are drained. It is said that nothing goes to waste in nature and everything has a purpose. Mud is no exception. In fact, mud serves many important purposes. First it is the home for a host of animals such as worms, frogs, snails, turtles, clams, and crayfish. Other animals love mud and enjoy nothing better than to wallow in it. Pigs, elephants, and rhinos use mud to cool down their bodies on a hot day and to protect their skins from pesky insect bites and overexposure to the sun. Mud is nature's first sunscreen. It is inexpensive too, although it lacks the aromatic scent to which we humans have grown accustomed.

Mud is also used in construction. Many people in the past and even today live in houses constructed essentially out of mud. But mud can also be a builder's bane. Clay soil, which can look and feel hard, readily turns into mud during heavy rains. Thus roads built of clay become mush when they get wet, making them virtually impassable. Construction workers learned long ago that buildings constructed on clay soil will eventually crack and even collapse without proper drainage. Mud's treachery is graphically displayed when mud slides sweep away entire villages. Mud is also used therapeutically. Mud used in this way is called peloid. The most popular peloids are peat pulps, sea mud, lake mud, and plant substances. Peloid procedures vary, but the most commonly used are peloid wraps, peloid baths, and peloid packs which are applied to the part of the body that is being treated. Peloid packs have been used for medicinal purposes in Europe for over 200 years to treat rheumatism, osteoarthritis, sciatica, and skin diseases.

Mud is also used in cosmetology. Face masks made of mud promise to revitalize your skin. They supposedly erase current wrinkles and prevent future wrinkles from taking up residence on your face. Mud is even used in the entertainment world. Watching adult men (or women) wrestling together in a vat of mud appeals to some people. (But mostly I say, "Yuck!")

Another significant use for mud is pottery. Pottery is made by forming clay (mud) into particular objects (such as figurines or vessels) and then heating them to extremely high temperatures. The heat causes a chemical reaction that strengthens and hardens the clay. The earliest known ceramic objects are Gravettian figurines such as those found in the modern-day Czech Republic. One Venus figurine dates back to 29,000–25,000 B.C. The earliest known pottery vessels are probably those found in Japan dating back to 10,500 B.C. For archaeologists and historians, the study of pottery is extremely important. Because pottery is so durable, even fragments can provide valuable clues about ancient civilizations.

Mud: home for animals as well as humans, road surface, medicinal relief, beauty enhancer, sunscreen, entertainment venue, and the basic ingredient for the world's pottery. That's a lot of uses for a substance many people consider yucky.

Reflection • Discussion

What has been my experience with mud?

Did your attitude toward mud change at all as you read this chapter? If so, how?

> We are the clay and you the potter:
> We are all the work of your hands. — ISAIAH 64:7

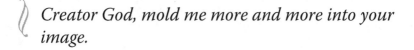 *Creator God, mold me more and more into your image.*

26

Rachel Carson

Truth is not only violated by falsehood; it may be outraged by silence.

❧ HENRI FREDERIC AMIEL

*A*s a child, I never saw any bluebirds where I lived in northeastern Ohio. Now, however, they are a fairly common sight. In fact, in recent years my father put up two bluebird houses on his property. In spring when I would stop in for a visit, I liked nothing better than to watch the parent birds flying in and out of the houses feeding their hungry broods. Upon occasion, I would tiptoe out to one of the birdhouses, gently unhook the lid, and peek inside. The sight of four or five tiny bluebirds crammed inside the nest delighted my soul. In fact, every time I spot a bluebird today, I thank God—and a woman named Rachel Carson.

Rachel Carson was born on a small farm near Pittsburgh, Pennsylvania on May 27, 1907. Her rural childhood gave her an appreciation of nature. Shy by nature, she loved to write poetry and even had a few things published while still a young girl. When Carson entered college, she intended to major in English and writing, but a sophomore biology course reawakened her fascination with nature. She eventually switched her major from English to marine biology.

After graduate studies, Carson taught science at several universities before being hired by the Bureau of Fisheries where she wrote and edited publications from cookbooks to scientific journals. She soon garnered a reputation for meticulous research and high standards of writing. When her father died, Carson moved back home to care for her mother. Several years later another family crisis occurred when her forty-year-old sister died leaving two young daughters. Carson took them in and raised them while still caring for her elderly mother.

Carson's first major book was *The Sea Around Us* which won the 1952 National Book Award and was on the New York Times best seller list for eighty-six weeks. It was followed three years later by *The Edge of the Sea*. But once again tragedy struck her family when her niece died leaving a five-year-old son. Carson adopted the boy and raised him too while still caring for her mother.

In January 1958, a woman named Olga Owens Huckins sent a letter to the *Boston Herald* and a copy to Carson. Huckins and her husband owned a bird sanctuary in Duxbury, Massachusetts. In her letter she described how the U.S. government was spraying the area with DDT in an effort to control the mosquitoes. As a result, hundreds of birds were dying. Huckins begged Carson to use her influence to investigate the wholesale use of pesticides and their impact on the environment.

For four years Carson painstakingly researched this topic. At first she tried to convince several magazines to run a series of articles on the topic, but they all declined. One editor told her they were not interested in running articles on such a "gloomy subject." So Carson was forced to turn her research into a book. During her writing, she had to stop several times to undergo chemotherapy for breast cancer. But in 1962 her book *Silent Spring* was published. The book soon became a best seller and was translated worldwide, making Carson the most famous woman scientist in the United States.

But not everyone was pleased with the book. Immediately the major U.S. chemical companies and their ally the U.S. Department of Agriculture launched an attack against the book. They labeled Carson a "hysterical woman" and disputed her data. One critic said if we listened to Carson, the planet would soon be overrun by insects, disease, and vermin. In the words of her biographer Paul Brooks, "She was questioning not only the indiscriminate use of poisons but the basic irresponsibility of an industrialized, technological society towards the natural world." Caron's book withstood the assaults of her critics. Eventually DDT was banned in the United States and elsewhere. Unfortunately Carson did not live to see this banning, for she died of breast cancer on April 14, 1964 at the age of fifty-six.

It is not an exaggeration to say that the modern environmental movement was born with *Silent Spring*. These many years later, the book continues to have an impact on readers. Writer Linda Lear sums up Carson's legacy in these words: "Her witness for the beauty and integrity of life continues to inspire new generations to protect the living world and all creatures."

That is why I give thanks to God and to Rachel Carson every time I see a bluebird.

Reflection • Discussion

How do I defend the beauty and integrity of life?

Have I ever had the courage to speak the truth despite opposition?

> Be brave and steadfast; have no fear or dread of them,
> for it is the Lord your God, who marches with you; he
> will never fail you or forsake you.   — DEUTERONOMY 31:6

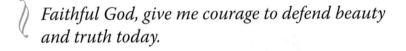

Faithful God, give me courage to defend beauty and truth today.

27

20 Fascinating Facts

Education is learning what you didn't even know you didn't know.

☞ DANIEL BOORSTIN

While many college students moan and groan about writing research papers, I actually liked writing them when I was a student. For one thing, I could write reasonably well. For another thing, I simply enjoyed doing research. I learned early on that when you are researching a particular topic, you come across a mountain of information you will never use in your paper. In fact, a completed paper is merely a tiny sliver of all the things you learned while writing it.

The same thing happens when writing a book. Take this one. As I delved into the research for this book, I discovered all kinds of things I knew I would not be able to use in the book. I decided, therefore, to dedicate this one reflection to a listing of a few of these facts. So here are twenty fascinating facts about nature I came across while looking for something else.

1. A ladybug can predict the weather six months in advance.
2. A flea can jump 14 to 16 feet horizontally. That is equivalent to a 6 foot human being jumping 200 feet.
3. An ostrich's eye is bigger than its brain.
4. A man in Virginia was struck by lightning four times and suffered these consequences: In 1942, he lost the nail on his big toe; in 1969, he lost his eyebrows; in 1970, his left shoulder was seared; in 1972, his hair was set on fire.
5. A cat has thirty-two muscles in each ear.
6. One day on Venus is equivalent to 243 earth days, while one day on Jupiter is only 9.9 earth hours long.
7. Tigers have striped skin as well as striped fur.
8. The human eye can differentiate seven million colors.
9. A male clownfish will change into a female if the latter dies.
10. Black lemurs use millipede secretions as a recreational drug and also to ward off mosquitoes.
11. A goldfish has a memory span of three seconds.
12. You will never find an eight-sided snowflake in nature.
13. A silicon chip a quarter of an inch square has the capacity of the original 1949 ENIAC computer which occupied a city block.
14. There are an estimated nine million species of insects yet to be discovered.
15. Taste buds in humans wear out every seven to ten days. Our body replaces them, but not as frequently after the age of forty-five.
16. In 1962, a coal mine under Centralia, Pennsylvania, acci-

dentally caught fire. It still burns today and, experts say, it might continue to burn for another century or two.

17. Fear of getting old is called gerontophobia; fear of chickens is called alektorophobia; fear of mothers-in-law is called pentheraphobia; and fear of the pope is called papaphobia.

18. When a dolphin sleeps, it shuts down only half of its brain, because its breathing is under voluntary control.

19. A squirrel fell sixteen stories down an air shaft is a New York City hotel and suffered only a nosebleed.

20. If the history of the universe were a calendar year, humans would first show up the last three minutes of December 31.

Reflection • Discussion

Are any of these facts particularly interesting to me?

Are there other fascinating facts about nature that I know?

What do these facts say to me about nature's Creator?

How precious to me are your designs, O God;
how vast the sum of them!
Were I to count, they would outnumber the sands;
To finish, I would need eternity.   — PSALM 139:17–18

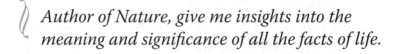 *Author of Nature, give me insights into the meaning and significance of all the facts of life.*

28

The Wind

*I will set my face to the wind and scatter
my seeds on high.*

ARABIAN PROVERB

You can tell which way the wind is blowing by looking at a herd of cows. Most often, cows will instinctively turn their fannies to the wind. They must find it annoying to have the wind blowing directly into their sad cow faces.

It's just the opposite with seagulls. The other day I saw a huge flock of seagulls on the beach standing at perfect attention and in perfect formation, all with their beaks pointing directly into the wind. Facing the wind makes sense for seagulls. It minimizes the ruffling of their feathers—something that must be irritating for them. Perhaps a strong wind could even harm their plumage. What good are bent feathers to a bird? If seagulls turned sideways to the wind, the poor things (weighing so little) would be blown right over. Kerplunk! No, seagulls must have learned thousands of years ago to make the most of their aerodynamically designed bodies and face every wind head on.

And what about me? Which direction do I face when strong winds blow in my life? Sometimes I wisely turn my backside to the gales, hunker down, and wait for them to subside. But other times, I learn to trust my design and face the wind head on. The important thing is discerning what kind of wind it is. Is it a wind for enduring or for confronting, a wind for my fanny or my face? Sometimes a good friend (even God) can help me with my discerning.

In Scripture, God is often associated with various kinds of wind. God appeared to Moses in the form of wind, fire, and storm on Mt. Sinai (Ex 19:16–19). In contrast, God came as a gentle breeze to the prophet Elijah in the cave (1 Kgs 19:11–12). On Pentecost, the Holy Spirit came as a "strong driving wind" which filled the entire house where the apostles were gathered (Acts 2:2). One lesson seems to be this: we must be open to all the ways God chooses to enter our lives—as raging storm, gentle breeze, or persistent gale.

Recently I was giving a retreat at the St. Benedict Center in Schuyler, Nebraska, in the heart of the prairie. I encouraged participants to go outside and engage in a dialogue with some aspect of nature. It turned out to be a very windy day, so several people wrote about the wind. One woman, Christine, noted that the wind's identity is influenced by what it touches or passes through. "Passing over water, the wind is cool," she wrote. "Whirling over the sun-warmed ground, it heats my face and back. Passing through the pines, it takes on an aroma." She then raised the questions, "What identity does the wind of God have as he passes through me? What do other people see, hear, and feel when they walk with me in life?" Good questions, I thought. Good questions.

Reflection • Discussion

Which direction have I turned for some of the winds in my life?

How did I know which direction was best?

What identity does the wind of God have as God passes through me?

> He awakened, rebuked the wind and the waves, and
> they subsided and there was calm. Then he asked them,
> "Where is your faith?" But they were filled with awe and
> amazement and said to one another, "Who then is this,
> who commands even the winds and the sea, and they
> obey him?" — LUKE 8:24‒25

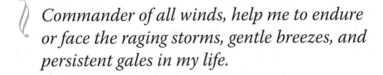 *Commander of all winds, help me to endure or face the raging storms, gentle breezes, and persistent gales in my life.*

29

The Newly Hatched Chicks

All beginnings are lovely.

 FRENCH PROVERB

O nce when I was feeling a little blue, I went over to the biology lab at the high school where I was teaching and played with the newly hatched chicks. There were six of them, little puffs of yellow fluff, cheeping and pecking continuously—except when they fell asleep—which they did quite readily and abruptly. Though the chicks were only a few days old, they were already beginning to get their pin feathers. Life is short for chickens, so they are programmed to mature quickly. Just seeing the chicks comforted me. They were so new, so fresh. I supposed they were a reminder to me that Life keeps starting over despite the reality of Death.

You would think Life would get tired of starting over all the time. You would think Life would eventually give up and say, "I'm never going to start over again. I'm never going to break out of a shell again, or burst forth from a seed again, or push up through the hard brown ground again. It's just too much work. And for what? I'm just going to die anyway."

But not Life. Not Silly Life. It keeps starting over. It keeps being born. It keeps being hatched. It keeps coming up even though Death is always right there waiting for it. Maybe Life knows something I sometimes forget: that Life is stronger than Death, or at least far more creative and persistent. Deal Death to Life and Life will only use Death as a nesting place for new life. You see it all the time: a soft chick emerging from a hard shell, a green shoot coming up through the crack in the black asphalt, a bird nesting in the hollow of a decaying tree, a crocus pushing up through the snow. Martin Luther said it well: "God has written the promise of the resurrection, not in books alone, but in every leaf in springtime."

One of my favorite life-from-death examples are the so-called "spring peepers," those small tree frogs found in abundance throughout the eastern United States and Canada. In his book *The Path: A One-Mile Walk through the Universe*, Chet Raymo describes the spring peepers in a nearby wetlands in this way: "Then comes the magic day in April when the entire surface of the water meadow begins to sing, the choiring of spring peepers, a hallelujah chorus in celebration of new life." He adds that the amazing fact about these peepers is that they were there in the water meadow all winter long, buried in the frozen mud. Raymo concludes, "Life doesn't come and go; life persists."

A theologian was asked to summarize the Bible in one sentence. He said, "I can do it in two words: Life wins." That's why I played with the newly hatched chicks in the biology lab that day. To remind myself of this great truth: Life goes on. Life persists. Life wins.

Reflection • Discussion

When I'm feeling blue, where do I go for comfort or encouragement?

Where in my life do I see life persisting or life winning?

[Jesus said]: "Jerusalem, Jerusalem...how many times I yearned to gather your children together, as a hen gathers her young under her wing, but you were unwilling."

— MATTHEW 23:37

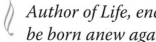 *Author of Life, encourage what is dead in me to be born anew again. And again.*

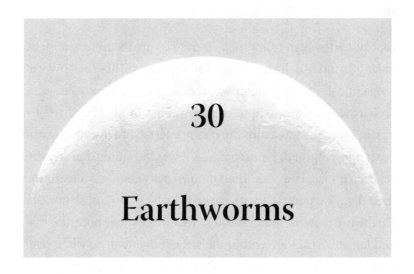

30

Earthworms

God is in the details.

☞ MIES VAN DER ROHE

A certain cartoon shows Noah standing on the deck of the ark with his son. Both of them look bored as they stare at all the water around them. Suddenly Noah says to his son, "I think I'll go fishing. Go get me one of those worms."

It's a good thing Noah didn't use one of his two worms for fishing, or human development would have been seriously jeopardized. For the truth is, the lowly earthworm plays a pivotal role in the fertility of earth's topsoil. And topsoil, some say, is the sustainer of civilization.

The earthworm is a cylindrical segmented worm of the Oligochaeta class in the phylum Anneldia. There are an estimated 2,200 species of such worms ranging in size from one inch to eleven feet. (That is not a typo!) The common American and European earthworm (*Lumbricus terrestris*) grows up to ten inches in length and usually has about 150 segments. These earthworms range in color from pale brown, reddish brown, to purple.

Earthworms are unique creatures. First of all, they have five hearts. I recently saw a film clip on the internet of a live earthworm's heart pumping, and, I must confess, it was intriguing. Earthworms eat in an unusual way too. Their mouth cavity connects directly into their digestive tract, so they have no throat, esophagus, or stomach. Earthworms are hermaphrodites. This means that both the male and female organs are within the same individual. So when referring to a particular earthworm, it is proper to say he/she.

Earthworms spend the majority of their lives beneath the earth. One reason they stay down there is because they need moisture to breathe through their skin. Direct sunlight can kill earthworms, so they don't come to the surface except on cloudy days or during the night. How many worms are beneath the earth doing their worm business? It is estimated that even poor soil can have as many as 250,000 worms per acre. Rich, farmland can have over 1,750,000 per acre! For the farmer, then, the weight of the earthworms under the soil can be as great as the weight of his livestock above the soil.

One cannot underestimate the supreme importance that earthworms play in soil fertility. They do this by converting organic materials (such as dead leaves, poop, and decaying animals) into valuable nutrients for the soil. In addition, through their constant burrowing, they mix the soil and create many little channels which facilitate aeration and drainage. Charles Darwin was so impressed with the work of earthworms that he said of them: "It may be doubted whether there are many other animals which have played so important a part in the history of the world, as have these lowly organized creatures."

Yet we humans tend to think disparagingly of earthworms. When we want to insult someone, we say to them, "You worm you!" as if being a worm was the worst possible thing anyone could be. Even the psalmist, to express his sense of isolation and dehumanization, cried out to God, "I am a worm" (Ps 22:7).

But a cursory look at earthworms—like this brief reflection—reminds us of the important contribution earthworms make to life on planet earth. Though they live mostly unseen beneath our feet, they are not to be trodden upon—either figuratively or practically. As we make attempts to recycle paper, aluminum, and glass, let us recall that earth's first true recyclers were and still are the earthworms.

Reflection • Discussion

Did I learn anything new about earthworms? If so, what?

How would the world be different without the work they do?

Is there any aspect of creation that I tend to disparage?

> How precious to me are your designs, O God;
>   how vast the sum of them!
> Were I to count, they would outnumber the sands;
>   to finish, I would need eternity." — PSALM 139:17–18

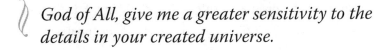

God of All, give me a greater sensitivity to the details in your created universe.

31

The Apple Orchard

*Reverence is the ritualization of wonder
and awe.*

☞ MATTHIAS NEUMAN, OSB

I often go into the apple orchard after supper—sometimes
with a friend or two, but most often alone. I love the orchard in all seasons, but especially now in early fall when
the branches are heavily laden with apples. The orchard is a different world from the one I ordinarily inhabit. Life in the orchard
has a distinctive tone, texture, and pace compared to life outside
the orchard. For one thing, the orchard is a very private place. All
those trees standing at attention in their neat little rows form a
protective shield from the stares or glares of the outside world.

But the orchard does more than provide privacy. It actually
alters some of the ordinary "rules" of daily living. For example,
you can be yourself in the orchard. Your age, occupation, title,

and responsibilities seem to dissolve when you enter an orchard. The trees welcome you into their sacred space. They invite you to plop down on the grass if you want to. A middle-aged college professor, for example, can flop on her back in the middle of the orchard if she feels like it. She can sing a song or leisurely count the apples above her head and no one will be scandalized— because no one will hear her or see her through the thick foliage of the trees.

And yes, you are free to eat the fruit of the orchard. No permission is required to help yourself to an apple, pear, or plum. It is still wrong, however, to steal a whole bag or basket of fruit as some passersby have done. But snitching a single apple or pear is fine. Just pluck it off the tree, spit on it, rub it against your sleeve, and bite into it. Crunch! Slurp! Mmmm! Is it just my imagination or does fruit always taste better the closer it is eaten to the tree that produced it? As I sit in the orchard munching on my apple, my thoughts turn to Eve. Yes, I say as I wipe some apple juice from my chin, I can see why she was tempted to eat that apple. Definitely.

In seasons other than fall, the apple orchard has a different feel to it. In spring, for example, as the trees break out into pink and white blossoms, the orchard becomes a veritable fairyland. The sight of all those blossoms coupled with their light fragrance is intoxicating. When a breeze kicks up and the flower petals begin to fall off the trees, you feel as if you are standing in the middle of a warm snow storm.

I have a fondness for the orchard even in winter. That's when the trees are stark naked. They look absolutely dead. It takes all the faith I can muster to believe that these same bare trees will once again produce blossoms, leaves, and so much fruit that their branches will sag under the weight. The orchard in winter is a symbol of hope to me. Hope hangs on to the certain knowledge that these bare trees have energy from the sun stored in their roots during the long, harsh winter. But in spring, this stored energy will rise up again into the tree's trunk and branches and burst forth into blossoms and leaves at the end of every single twig.

Reflection • Discussion

What has been my experience with orchards?

What are some of the places where I can go to relax and be myself?

What season of the year do I like best? Why?

> As an apple tree among the trees of the woods,
>   so is my lover among men.
> I delight to rest in his shadow.
>   and his fruit is sweet to my mouth.   — SONGS 2:3

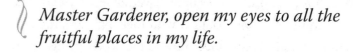 *Master Gardener, open my eyes to all the fruitful places in my life.*

32

The Polio Vaccine

The cosmic religious experience is the strongest and most noble driving force of scientific research.

☛ ALBERT EINSTEIN

*I*t was the summer of 1955. Disneyland opened, the first McDonalds started selling burgers, Rosa Parks refused to give up her seat on the bus, and people had great hopes that the new Salk vaccine would stop the spread of polio. It was the summer eighteen-year-old Dan Miller, fresh out of high school with a college scholarship awaiting him, was planning his future which he hoped would include becoming a teacher, a pilot, a guitar player, a husband, and a father. But one hot day, after working outside for several hours, Dan didn't feel well. Thinking he had the flu, he went to bed. Within a couple of days he was in a hospital paralyzed, having lost the use of both his arms and his legs. Dan Miller was a victim of polio. The Salk vaccine, which was being distributed throughout the United States that summer, had not yet made it to his small town of Pateros, Washington (population 643). Miller says, "I missed the vaccine by three weeks."

Anyone who grew up in the first half of the twentieth century remembers the terror associated with the word polio. Photographs of children with bent arms, or cumbersome leg braces, or (worse yet) being confined to an iron lung were everywhere. One of the great ironies of the disease is this: in the nineteenth century, when sanitation conditions were poor in the United States, children often built up a natural immunity to the disease, so polio was relatively rare. But when sanitation conditions improved greatly in the twentieth century, polio became rampant.

Since there was no cure for polio, the "Great Race" for a vaccine began in earnest in 1910. Jonas Salk, a young man from New York City, was studying to be a doctor in the 1930s. By chance, he was led into conducting research—a work he came to enjoy. In 1942, he, along with several others, developed an influenza vaccine for the U.S. Army. In 1947 he set his sights on finding a polio vaccine. Five years later, Salk had developed a vaccine that eventually proved to be ninety-nine percent effective.

The mass polio vaccination process began in the United States in April 1955. In 1962, another researcher, Albert Sabin, invented an oral vaccine which made the distribution of the vaccine considerably easier. So effective was the polio vaccine that the number of polio cases decreased from 350,000 worldwide in 1988 to less than 2,000 in 2006. Today whole areas of the world are polio free including the Americas, China, Australia, the Western Pacific countries, and Europe. There is hope that some day the disease may be completely eradicated—as was smallpox in 1979.

As a young man, Jonas Salk was not particularly interested in medicine. He said, "I was more interested in things human, in the human side of nature." He devoted himself to medical research because he wished "to be of some help to humankind." American folklorist Zora Neale Hurston says this about research: "Research is formalized curiosity. It is poking and prying with a purpose." Salk had a noble purpose for his work. By conducting scientific research day after day in his lab, he indeed benefited all of humankind.

Which brings us back to Dan Miller. To think of him as a "victim" of polio would be erroneous, for Dan went on to regain the use of one arm and fifteen percent of his leg muscles. Though he gets around in a scooter, he did realize his dream of becoming a schoolteacher—plus a coach and principal. He eventually married and today is the father of three grown children. Now Dan is the author of a best-selling book, *Living, Laughing, and Loving Life* and he tours the country as a highly successful motivational speaker. And yes, he plays the guitar and he owns and flies his own airplane. He plays golf too and recently shot a hole in one.

Dan Miller reminds his audiences, "If you're going through hell, keep going." He also says, "Heartache, pain, suffering, and grief come to everyone. Pain is inevitable, but misery is optional and joy is a choice."

Reflection • Discussion

What has been my experience with regard to diseases such as polio?

Do I agree with Dan Miller that "pain is inevitable, but misery is optional and joy is a choice"? Why or why not?

> Peter said, "I have neither gold nor silver, but what I do have I give you: in the name of Jesus Christ the Nazorean, [rise and] walk." Then Peter took him by the right hand and raised him up, and immediately his feet and ankles grew strong. — ACTS 3:6–7

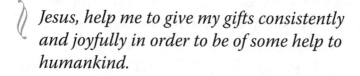

Jesus, help me to give my gifts consistently and joyfully in order to be of some help to humankind.

33

Weird Nature

*As humans our tendency is to define,
grab, control, dictate, possess, cling, buy,
and sell. Mystery, being pure gift, eludes
our manipulation by these potentially
destructive tendencies.*

                      ☙ SISTER JEANNE KOMA

*A*while ago the Discovery channel ran a series called "Weird Nature" which explored some of the strange behaviors of various animals. One show featured bizarre breeding behaviors. It featured the male bowerbird of Australia that goes to great lengths to fashion an elaborate nest from twigs, leaves, and moss in order to attract a mate. To add to the appeal of the nest, the bird decorates it with all kinds of ornaments such as feathers, pebbles, berries, and shells. He sometimes even steals shiny things from humans (coins, keys, jewelry) to adorn his nest and win the heart of a lady bower-bird.

Other animals strut or dance to attract a partner. The male peacock fans his splendid tail and struts around like there is no tomorrow in his attempt to impress a female. Some birds actually dance. One of the best bird dancers is the male red-capped mani-kin who does a very good imitation of Michael Jackson's moon-walk. Male and female scorpions dance together during court-ship. They link claws and dance a primitive form of the samba.

Some animals have devised ingenious ways to provide child-care for their offspring. The male Siamese fighting fish blows bubbles that rise to the surface of the water. Once he has mated with a female, he picks up the fertilized eggs in his mouth one at a time and spits them into the bubbles for safe-keeping. Other fish are mouth-brooders. The female cichlids of Africa and South America, for example, carry their fertilized eggs in their mouths for protection. Even after the eggs have hatched, the young fish still spend much of the time in their mother's mouth, except when they go outside to play or forage.

Some animals have developed strange eating habits. Take the golden eagles of Greece. These birds love tortoise meat. But even the powerful beak and talons of the eagle are no match for a tor-toise tucked inside its impenetrable shell. So what have the eagles learned to do? They snatch tortoises off the ground, carry them high into the air, and drop them onto rocky ground, thus break-ing open their shells.

The archer fish is a regular Annie Oakley when it comes to securing food. The fish fills its mouth with water and uses it like a water pistol to shoot down insects crawling on the vegetation hanging over the water. The aim of the archer fish is so accurate it can hit its target seven feet away!

Then there are the strange ways animals defend themselves. The three-banded armadillo, with its armor plating, just curls up into a perfect, invincible ball. Hedgehogs and porcupines have spiny needles to deter predators. The skunk possesses a unique weapon: a mace-like spray which it can shoot several yards away. A skunk's spray is so potent that a direct hit in the eye can cause temporary blindness. Even a hit that misses its target can cause a stench so awful it can induce vomiting.

In looking at "weird nature," a question arises. When is a certain behavior weird and when is it not? We humans tend to think that the weirdest animals are those who behave least like us. We conclude, therefore, that carrying babies in your mouth is weird, or feeding your offspring regurgitated food is weird. But, paradoxically, we sometimes label animals weird if their behavior is similar to ours. We find it weird that the bowerbird gives gifts during courtship or our cat leaves us a dead mouse on our doorstep, for perhaps we like to think that gift giving is a unique human behavior.

Another question arises: would other animals think we humans are weird? Probably so. They would think it weird that we walk upright on only two feet. No other animal does this—not even monkeys, chimps, or apes which all lean forward when they walk, sometimes using their hands or knuckles for support. Animals would think it weird that we humans have no protective fur, feathers, scales, or armor. All we have is skin with a measly bit of hair here and there. As a result, we are very susceptible to temperature change and very vulnerable to penetration.

Animals might even pity us. The cheetah would pity us for not being able to run fast, the dolphin because we have no fins. The eagle would lament our poor eyesight, the basset hound our pitiful excuse for a nose. Most mammals would say it is too bad that we have such large brains too, for they make human childbirth so difficult and painful.

It is probably good for us humans to reflect on behaviors we deem weird. For one thing, our reflection can give us a greater awareness of our strong links with the rest of the animal world. It can also bestow on us a richer appreciation of the wide diversity among animals. This awareness and appreciation can lead us to a greater tolerance and even love for diversity wherever we encounter it—even in other human beings.

Reflection • Discussion

Of all the animal behaviors described in this chapter, which do I find most weird? Why?

What behaviors in humans have I labeled weird?

How tolerant am I of diversity?

How varied are your works, Lord!
In wisdom you have wrought them all.   — PSALM 104:24

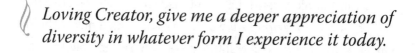 *Loving Creator, give me a deeper appreciation of diversity in whatever form I experience it today.*

34

The Desert

*Go into the desert, and the desert will
teach you everything.*

 DESERT FATHER ABBA MOSES

A good friend recently gave me a CD/DVD program entitled *Dunes, Canyons, and Desert Oasis.* Produced by Global Television, the CD contains seventy-eight minutes of spellbinding original music. The companion DVD contains all the music coupled with spectacular pictures from around the world. These pictures, says the cover jacket, feature "the serenity of sun-drenched Saharan landscapes, the visually impressive imagery of nature's handwork in the creation of canyons, and the cooling refreshment of a desert oasis." I use the DVD not only for my own personal prayer, but also for retreats that I give. It is an audio-visual tribute to the striking beauty found in the harshness of a desert landscape.

Deserts encompass one-fifth of the earth's total surface, or one-third of the earth's land surface. What exactly is a desert? Simply put, it is a place with a "moisture deficit." Translated into measurable data, that means it is an area with a rainfall of less than ten inches per year. What is the world's largest desert? (Be careful. This is a trick question.) If you said the Sahara Desert (like I did), you are wrong. The largest desert is the Antarctic Desert which is roughly 5.4 million square miles. (Not all deserts are hot.) The Sahara in northern Africa comes is second (3.32 million square miles) and the Arabia Desert is third (900,000 square miles).

When we think of deserts we usually think of hot and dry places. But that's only one kind of desert. There are three other kinds called semiarid, coastal, and cold. Deserts also have the reputation for supporting very little life, but a closer examination shows that deserts actually have a high biodiversity. Deserts support life forms such as ground-hugging shrubs, cacti, insects, jack rabbits, birds, lizards, snakes, toads, kangaroo rats, and mice of all kinds. Despite this biodiversity, though, most deserts are pretty hostile for humans. Yet some people have called the desert their home for thousands of years: Bedouins, the Tuareg Tribe, and Pueblo people, for example.

Deserts often contain valuable mineral deposits such as gypsum, salts, and borates, an essential ingredient in the manufacture of glass, enamel, water softeners, agricultural chemicals, and pharmaceuticals. Deserts are also ideal places for the natural preservation of artifacts and fossils and, more recently, old airplanes.

One of the most controversial uses of a desert this past century was as a testing ground for nuclear weapons. The first atomic bomb was detonated in the Northern Chihuahuan Desert in New Mexico at 5:29 AM on July 16, 1945. Why was this area chosen as the place to build and test the atomic bomb? Primarily because it was sparsely populated (at least by humans) and it was a desert. Only a desert.

Christianity has had a long love affair with the desert. We recall how Jesus began his public ministry with a forty-day foray into the desert. Early Christianity, beginning in the third century, gave rise to groups of hermits, ascetics, and monks, both men and women, who went into the desert seeking to find God. These figures, often called Desert Fathers and Mothers, soon gained a reputation for holiness and wisdom. Their desert experience was said to purge them of selfish desires, thus opening their hearts more readily to the Divine.

Metropolitan Gerasimos of the Greek Orthodox Archdiocese of America, recently spoke about the beauty and impact of the desert as he relocated himself from Massachusetts to California to assume his new responsibilities. He said, "In the desert, everything is sharpened and intensified: the beauty of the land is not in smooth contours, but in stark, rugged outlines and jagged edges; not in green hillsides, but in the vivid red and copper hues of the earth. The desert plants are not lush, but they are full of intensity....When the rain falls, the desert floor is covered with bursts of brilliant colors as the wildflowers bloom and clothe the land in splendor." He summarizes the impact of the desert in these words: "The desert is the place of intensification."

Reflection • Discussion

What has been my experience of the desert?

Did I learn anything new in this chapter?

I will read about Jesus' forty days in the desert (Mt 4:1–11) and see what it has to teach me today.

> Then Jesus was led by the Spirit into the desert to be
> tempted by the devil. — MATTHEW 4:1

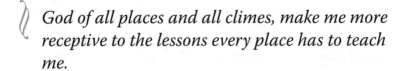

God of all places and all climes, make me more receptive to the lessons every place has to teach me.

35

Rediscovering Fire

Set your life on fire.
Seek those who fan your flames.

∾ RUMI

*T*his is what I know about fire: Fire is ambivalent. It destroys; it heals. It consumes life; it sustains life. It is terrifying to behold. It is beautiful to behold.

Almost all ancient peoples have legends about where fire came from. When we read these primitive stories, we are struck by their uncanny similarity. The ancient Greeks said, for example, that a certain Titan by the name of Prometheus stole fire from the gods and gave it to poor helpless humankind. As a punishment for his crime, Prometheus was chained to a rock by Zeus where, every day, a vulture came and tore out his regenerating liver. In the Rig Veda of the Hindu tradition, the hero Matarisvan recovers fire which the gods had hidden from humankind. A Polynesian myth

117

says that the great hero Maui stole fire from the fingernails of the Fire-goddess, Mahuika, barely escaping with his life in the process. And the ancient Cherokee myth says that when Possum and Buzzard failed to steal fire, Grandmother Spider used her web to sneak into the land of the night and stole fire by hiding it in a clay pot.

Humans did not invent fire. Fire had been on planet earth for at least 400 million years. But our human ancestors "stole" fire from nature, learned to control it, and tamed it for their use. Evidence that fire was used for cooking by these primitive peoples in South Africa goes back 1½ million years. Fire kept humans alive when temperatures dipped dangerously low. Fire made it possible for them to migrate to colder climates in their endless quest for food. And fire's use for cooking was a key ingredient in the fight against disease. Little wonder that some anthropologists say that the ability to control fire is one of humankind's greatest achievements.

Fire remains just as critical today as it was in ancient times. An estimated eighty percent of the power used in the world today comes from setting fuel aflame—whether that fuel is wood, petroleum, natural gas, coal, or some other combustible. Says one scientist, "In its broadest sense, fire is used by nearly every human being on earth in a controlled setting every day." The woman in Uganda crouched over her small fire, the man in France driving his internal combustion car, and the child in China turning on the light switch in the dark room are all, in essence, relying on the power of fire.

In sacred Scripture, fire plays a significant role. Abraham resists the worship of Moloch, the god of fire, who demands child sacrifice (Gn 22). Moses one day curiously ambles over to check out a burning bush and encounters instead the living God (Ex 3—4:17). When God leads the Hebrews through the desert, God appears as a column of cloud by day and a pillar of fire by night (Ex 13:21). When Jeremiah is tempted to abandon his prophetic mission, he cries, "I will speak in (God's) name no more." His resolve is short-lived, for he soon breaks down and says, "But then it becomes like a fire burning in my heart, / imprisoned in my bones; / I grow weary holding it in" (Jer 20:9).

In the New Testament, Jesus describes his mission in terms of fire when he says, "I have come to set earth on fire, and how I wish it were already blazing" (Lk 12:49). When the Holy Spirit descends on the apostles in the upper room on Pentecost, it is as "tongues of fire" (Acts 2:3). And the author of the letter to the Hebrews says simply, "Our God is a consuming fire" (Heb 12:29).

Fire, then, is richly symbolic. Most often it stands for love, but it can also represent love's opposite, hatred. Teilhard de Chardin was a twentieth-century paleontologist, poet, and priest. He looked at the universe through the eyes of a mystic, beholding the presence of Christ in everything. Teilhard was fascinated by fire, seeing it as the source of warmth and light, with energy to transform and fuse everything. But he was also keenly aware of fire's destructive capabilities—most terrifyingly the possibility of a nuclear holocaust. According to Teilhard, only the fire of love was capable of extinguishing the fire of hatred. He wrote this magnificent and hope-filled description of love's power: "The day will come when, after harnessing the ether, the winds, the tides, and gravitation, we shall harness for God the energies of love. And on that day, for the second time in the history of the world, [humankind] will have discovered fire."

Reflection • Discussion

What has been my experience with fire—both negative and positive?

What if anything intrigues me about fire?

What do I think of the final quotation by Teilhard de Chardin?

> John answered them all, saying, "I am baptizing you
> with water, but one mightier than I is coming. I am not
> worthy to loosen the thongs of his sandals. He will bap-
> tize you with the holy spirit and fire."   — LUKE 3:16

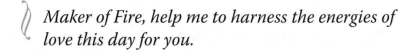

Maker of Fire, help me to harness the energies of love this day for you.

36

Amazing Maize

The Christian is like the ripening corn; the riper he grows, the more he bends his head.

☞ A.B. GUTHRIE, JR.

Corn, or maize as it is called in much of the world, was first domesticated in central Mexico about 9,000 years ago. Over time it spread north and south throughout the American continents and east into the Caribbean. When Christopher Columbus landed on Cuba in 1493, he found corn there and took it back with him to Spain. Today corn is grown on every continent of the world except Antarctica. In fact, more corn (by weight) is produced each year worldwide than any other grain.

Corn comes in a variety of colors: blackish, bluish gray, red, white, and yellow. Modern hybrids have bigger ears, grow faster, survive in chillier temperatures, and are generally more pest resistant than older varieties. Sweet corn is distinct from field corn.

It is a genetic variation of corn that accumulates more sugar and less starch—hence its name.

The corn plant is a wonder to behold. First of all, when corn is planted, its initial growth is slow. But once a plant has reached twenty-four inches in height, its growth is amazingly fast. There's an old saying that says "you can hear the corn grow." It's almost true, for, during one warm summer night, a corn stalk can grow three to four inches. The corn plant is made up of several parts. The ear of corn, which consists of the kernels of corn wrapped securely in several layers of leaves (or husks), is the female reproductive organ of the plant. Attached to each separate kernel is a thin thread called silk. The male reproductive organ of the plant is the tassel situated at the apex of the stem. The tassel produces two to five million grains of pollen to fertilize the plant. Each silk needs one grain of pollen to produce one kernel of corn. The tassel on one stalk must pollinate the silk on other stalks of corn planted nearby. Since the average ear of corn has between 400 and 800 kernels, pollination is quite a feat. To facilitate pollination, corn is planted in bunches—usually several rows side by side. In the end, each corn plant usually produces a single ear of corn.

Corn used to be harvested by hand, a slow and painstaking job. But today we have huge machines called combines that can harvest a crop of corn the size of a football field in minutes. One combine holds about 200 bushels of corn. (One combine also costs about $240,000!)

Corn as we know it today would not exist if it weren't for humans. In fact it is accurate to say that corn is a human invention. This means it doesn't exist in the wild. It can exist only if it is planted and cared for by us.

About fifty-eight percent of the corn produced in the United States today is used as food for animals. The other 42% is used for food for humans and in the production of a whole host of other products. A recent survey of 10,000 items in the grocery store showed that 2,500 of them contained corn in one form or another. A popular Web site for children lists "a zillion" uses for corn. Although that's an exaggeration, nonetheless, even a partial listing of the many uses of corn is impressive. Corn is used in adhesives, soft drinks, dry cell batteries, beer, wallpaper, candy, spark plugs, ketchup, latex paint, chewing gum, peanut butter, disposable diapers, cardboard, potato chips, carpets, shoe polish, whiskey, soaps, toothpaste, aspirin, yogurt, and thousands of other items.

Corn is also used as fuel. Some people simply burn feed corn for heating. But corn is also seen as a major player in our attempts to reduce our dependency on oil for fuel. Ethanol, which is made from corn, is an additive in gasoline that reduces petroleum consumption. Currently there is an intense debate about using corn for fuel. American farmers are now planting more and more corn to be used for fuel instead of food. One unintentional and negative consequence of this shift has been a sharp rise in food prices as well as food shortages in some countries. The question remains: how can we find creative ways to reduce oil consumption by using corn while still feeding people all over the world?

Reflection • Discussion

What has been my experience with corn?

Did I learn anything new in this chapter?

Where do I stand on the debate between corn as fuel and corn as food?

> The pastures are clothed with flocks,
> the valleys blanketed with grain;
> they cheer and sing for joy.   — PSALM 65:14

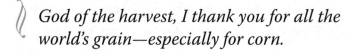 *God of the harvest, I thank you for all the world's grain—especially for corn.*

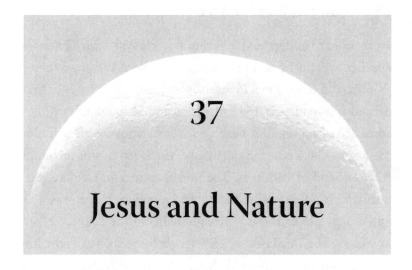

37

Jesus and Nature

Notice the ravens....Notice how the flowers grow.

☞ JESUS

*I*n his article entitled "Ecology and Religion," Sean McDonagh, SCC, bemoans the fact that, in the contemporary discussion of ecology, so little attention is played to Jesus' life and teachings. He writes, "Whilst the text on (ecology) posters might come from Chief Seattle's address or the Indian poet Tagore, I have never seen a quotation from the Bible or a reference to the words of Jesus."

Father McDonagh has a point. He raises these questions: What role does nature play in the life and teachings of Jesus? Does Jesus have anything to say about our current environmental concerns? This chapter will explore those questions.

In order to understand the natural world with which Jesus was familiar, we must first know something about the geography of Palestine. In Jesus' time, Palestine was a narrow rectangular strip of land approximately 150 miles long and 50 to 60 miles wide. It consisted of mountains, desert, rich farmland, the river Jordan, the Sea of Galilee in the north, and the Dead Sea in the south. It was a land of contrasts. The northern region, Galilee, was a lush land of rolling hills. The southern region, Judea, was a dry and craggy place. There were mountains in the country as well as valleys. The Dead Sea, at 1378 feet below sea level, is the lowest place on earth. Although Jesus was said to be born in Judea (Bethlehem) and he died in Judea (outside Jerusalem), he spent most of his life in Galilee.

Jesus was close to nature. He spent a great deal of time outdoors. In fact, most of his teaching was done outside. As Father McDonagh writes, "His teaching ministry was not carried out in buildings, in synagogues, or in the temple, but in the cathedral of nature." Nature was an integral part of his public ministry. Before embarking on his ministry, for example, Jesus spent forty days alone in the wilderness (Mt 4:1–11); he called his first disciples as he walked along the shores of the Sea of Galilee (Mk 4:18–22); he returned often to the hills to pray (Mt 17:1); he gave his most important discourses in the mountains (Mt 5:1–7); he cured many people outdoors (Lk 7:11–17; Lk 9:37–43; Mt 8:28–34; Mk 6:53–56); he multiplied loaves in a "deserted place" (Mt 14:13–21); he was transfigured before three of his disciples on "a high mountain" (Mk 9:2–8); and he sought refuge in a garden of olive trees immediately before his arrest and execution (Lk 22:39).

Many of Jesus' parables are centered on nature. He speaks of mustard seeds, grains of wheat, grapevines, fig trees, lilies, water, wheat, and weeds. His life and teachings are sprinkled with animals such as birds, sheep, goats, dogs, camels, fish, mother hens, doves, snakes, donkeys, foxes, and wolves. He is familiar with various processes of nature: yeast causing dough to rise, grapes fermenting into tasty wine, tiny seeds germinating into fruitful plants, a woman giving birth to a child, fertilizer enriching the soil, clouds bringing much needed rain, life yielding to death, and death yielding to new life. He sees these processes of the natural world as parallel to the workings of the spiritual world.

Jesus not only centers his parables on nature, he identifies himself with the natural elements such as a vine (Jn 15:1), bread (Jn 6:48), water (Jn 4:13–14), and light (Jn 8:12). He is well aware of the darker side of nature, too: a man convulsing in the synagogue (Mk 1:29), terrible diseases such as leprosy (Lk 5:12–16), the vagaries of weather and soil (Mt 13:1–9), the futility involved in fishing all night and catching nothing (Jn 21:1–6), the destructive power of a violent storm (Lk 8:22–25).

If we look at the gospels, we also see that Jesus possesses a contemplative attitude toward nature. He notices things. He sees into them. And he encourages his followers to share this contemplative attitude when he says things like, "Notice the ravens... Notice how the flowers grow" (Lk 12:24, 27). Jesus shows his reverence for nature also when he calls his disciples to travel lightly upon the earth. They are to "take nothing for the journey, neither walking stick, nor sack, nor food, nor money, and let no one take a second tunic" (Lk 9:3). Jesus continuously warned against the danger of attachment to possessions and power—an attachment that lies at the core of our environmental crisis. His primary mandate can be summarized in these three words, "Love one another." And one of the primary ways we show this love is by the sharing of our goods and ourselves with others (Lk 10:29–37).

Jesus never wrote a book about ecology. Yet our contemporary ecological movement will succeed only: 1) if is rooted in a contemplative attitude toward nature, 2) if we learn not only to travel more lightly, but to live more lightly by living with less, and 3) if we learn to love one another by sharing more equitably all the resources on planet earth.

Reflection • Discussion

What strikes me the most about the role nature plays in the life and teachings of Jesus?

Do I share Jesus' contemplative attitude toward the natural world?

How lightly am I traveling on earth?

> [Jesus said]: "Do not be afraid any longer, little flock, for your Father is pleased to give you the kingdom."
>
> — LUKE 12:32

 Jesus, give me eyes to see God's loving presence everywhere.

Index

(The number indicates the number of the reflection)